PRESIDENTS AND FIRST LADIES

OF THE UNITED STATES

DORANNE JACOBSON

SMITHMARK
PUBLISHERS INC.

16 East 32nd Street, New York, NY 10016

DEDICATION

This book is dedicated to my grandparents, Robert L. Novy and Elsie B. Novy, who took me on my first visit to
Washington, D.C., and to the members of my family who shared Washington with me later: Russell E. Wilson, Dorothy Novy Wilson,
Patti Wilson, Jacqueline Wilson, Pamela Wilson, Wendy Wilson, Jerome Jacobson, Laurie Jacobson, and Joshua Jacobson.

ACKNOWLEDGMENTS

I wish to express appreciation for the use of the collections at the Lincoln Library, Springfield, Illinois, and
Butler Library, Columbia University, New York. I also thank Jerome Jacobson for his editorial suggestions.

This edition published by SMITHMARK Publishers Inc.,
16 East 32nd Street, New York, NY 10016

SMITHMARK books are available for bulk purchase
for sales promotion and premium use.
For details write or call the manager of special sales,
SMITHMARK Publishers Inc.,
16 East 32nd Street, New York, NY 10016; (212) 532-6600.

This book was designed and produced by
Todtri Productions Limited
P.O. Box 20058
New York, NY 10023-1482

Printed and bound in Singapore

Library of Congress Card Catalog Number 95-067763

ISBN 0-8317-8166-8

Author: Doranne Jacobson

Producer: Robert Tod
Book Designer: Mark Weinberg
Production Coordinator: Heather Weigel
Project Editor: Edward Douglas
Typesetting: Command-O, NYC

PICTURE CREDITS

Art Resource, New York 8-9
Jean Buldain/Picture Perfect USA 21
Jimmy Carter Library 117 (left & right)
James Colburn/Photoreporters 124
Dwight D. Eisenhower Library 98, 99, 100 (top & bottom), 101 (top & bottom)
Gerald R. Ford Library 115 (top & bottom)
Paul Gero/Nawrocki Stock Photo 118, 120, 121 (top & bottom), 122, 123 (top)
John F. Kennedy Library 102, 103, 104, 105 (right)
Illinois State Historical Library 53, 55 (top)
Robert Knudsen/LBJ Library 107
Library of Congress 32 (top), 58
Dodie Miller/Picture Perfect USA 77 (top)
National Archives/Nixon Presidential Materials 111, 112 (top & bottom), 113
National Gallery of Art, Washington, D.C. 13
National Museum of American Art, Washington, D.C./Art Resource, New York 29 (top), 49 (bottom)
The National Portrait Gallery, Washington, D.C./Art Resource, New York 4, 12, 17, 26, 28, 30, 36, 41 (bottom), 48, 56, 63, 66 (top), 70, 79
Nawrocki Stock Photo 10, 11 (top & bottom), 14, 15 (top & bottom), 16, 19, 20, 22, 23, 25, 27 (top), 29 (bottom), 32, 33,
37 (top & bottom), 38, 39 (top & bottom), 40 (top & bottom), 42, 43 (top & bottom), 46, 52, 54, 57 (top & bottom),
60, 61 (top & bottom), 64, 65 (bottom), 67, 68 (top), 69, 71 (top), 72, 73, 76, 77 (bottom), 78, 80, 81, 82, 83 (top & bottom),
84 (top & bottom), 86, 87 (top & bottom), 88, 93, 97 (bottom) 105 (left), 106, 109, 110, 114, 116, 119
New York City Art Commission 34
New York Public Library Picture Collection 47 (top), 59 (top), 65 (top), 71 (bottom)
North Wind Picture Archives 5, 6-7, 24, 27 (bottom), 31, 47 (bottom), 49 (top), 55 (bottom), 59 (bottom), 62 (top & bottom), 66 (bottom), 68 (bottom)
Yoichi R. Okamoto/LBJ Library 108 (top)
Mark Reinstein/Photoreporters 125 (top)
Franklin D. Roosevelt Library 89, 90, 91, 92 (top & bottom)
Theodore Roosevelt Collection/Harvard College Library 75 (bottom)
Ede Rothaus 75 (top)
Sangamon Valley Collection, Lincoln Library, Springfield, Illinois 50
Bob Self/Silver Image 123 (bottom)
Kevin Shields/New England Stock Photo 18
Scott T. Smith/Picture Perfect USA 108 (bottom)
Harry S. Truman Library 94, 95, 96, 97 (top)
White House Historical Association 35 (top & bottom), 74, 85
Kevin Wisniewski/Silver Image 125 (bottom)

CONTENTS

Right:
George Washington brought the Colonies through the Revolutionary War to create a republic dedicated to justice and equality. In 1814, Dolley Madison rescued this priceless portrait by Gilbert Stuart from the burning White House. Today the portrait hangs in the East Room and is the only object remaining from the mansion's earliest occupancy in 1800.

INTRODUCTION

Americans have been fascinated with their Presidents and First Ladies since the nation's birth. Without a royal family on whom to focus their attention, Americans have viewed their elected leaders and their families with feelings of admiration, affection, disdain, dependence, sympathy, criticism, and understanding. America's presidents and their wives have sprung from a wide variety of backgrounds and have shown an equally wide variety of character traits. Every detail of appearance and conduct, both public and private, has been the object of intense scrutiny and judgment by the American public.

America's political process demands such scrutiny—every four years the people are entrusted with the right and duty to choose their national leader, either returning a president to office or selecting another chief executive to carry on the nation's democratic tradition. Thus, every few years, there is a whole new cast of characters playing out a human drama at the White House, shaping and responding to an ever-changing larger national drama.

The presidents of the United States have all been men of European descent, some from elite families, others from more humble backgrounds. Many of America's earliest presidents were from Virginia, a land of gentleman farmers and intellectual accomplishments. As the nation matured, the geographic center of the presidency gradually moved further West, where settlers with calloused hands had little time for reading the classics. Later presidents came from Missouri, Texas and California—regions barely known to residents of the original thirteen colonies. Many presidential couples have had ties to New England.

Some presidents were well-educated and brilliant, such as Thomas Jefferson, while others like Andrew Johnson struggled with educational handicaps. The presidential wives have taken on a wide range of roles, some flamboyant and regal in satin and ostrich plumes, others plain in black bonnets, some shy and invisible, others publicly active in social causes. Early on, Abigail Adams, wife of the second president, brought the notion of the "power of doing good" to the role of president's wife. In general, the First Ladies have been much more powerful, both publicly and behind the scenes, than has been widely recognized.

Above: The White House, at 1600 Pennsylvania Avenue, has been both presidential home and symbol of presidential power for nearly two centuries. In this 1877 view, visitors approach the North Portico facing Pennsylvania Avenue, paying social and political calls as President Grant's term ends and President Hayes' begins.

What each of these presidential families had was a full life—a dramatic story of living in a rapidly-changing nation, facing challenges, and sharing their lives with the country. Virtually all Presidents and First Ladies, whatever their disparate backgrounds, seem to have shared a conscientious desire to do what was good for the family and for the nation. A sense of honestly trying to do the right thing—differently perceived by different leaders—has been almost a constant quality of occupants of the White House.

Triumph and tragedy, joy and despair have all gone hand in hand with the presidency. The early presidential families lived when death often struck suddenly, harvesting both young and old. Like other Americans, First Families suffered the premature deaths of parents, spouses, children, and friends. Notions of hygiene were rudimentary, and medical practice was still relatively primitive. With no miracle drugs at hand, pneumonia, tuberculosis, typhus, cholera, smallpox, and other killer diseases struck at the White House even as they did at the humbler dwellings of ordinary citizens. And then there were the assassinations, cruelly striking down nearly a tenth of America's presidents in their prime, leaving the nation weeping in sorrow time and time again.

The setting for activities of presidential families has been the White House, official residence and office for the nation's leader and his kin, situated in the heart of America's capital city. Washington, D.C. developed as a carefully planned capital, laid out by the brilliant but quixotic French architect Pierre Charles L'Enfant at the behest of George Washington, who shared his vision of a beautiful city rising from the banks of the Potomac River. Together, Washington and L'Enfant walked the wooded hills and marshy ground, personally selecting sites for the Capitol building, the broad avenues, and the President's House, as it was then designated.

In 1792, the winner of the competition for the design of the President's House was announced: James Hoban, an Irish immigrant. His plans for a simple European-style three-storied boxlike structure, handsome and dignified, became the basis for the Executive Mansion, whose construction George Washington intermittently supervised. Unfortunately, Washington died before either the capital or residence could be completed.

The second president, John Adams, was the first to move into the mansion, still very much unfinished. On November 1, 1800, his first night in the cold, damp house, Adams wrote to his wife, "I pray Heaven to bestow the best of Blessings on this House and all that shall hereafter inhabit it. May none but honest and wise Men ever rule under this roof." More than 130 years later, this auspicious sentiment was carved on the mantel of the State Dining Room at the request of Franklin Roosevelt.

Over the life of the nation, the White House has undergone a vast number of changes. The British burned it in 1814, leaving only its exterior sandstone walls standing. It was rebuilt grandly, with porticoes and wings added at various times. Many presidential families arranged renovations, repairs, remodeling, and, in President Harry Truman's time, reconstruction. Decorating schemes have ranged from copies of European palatial rooms in the French style to cluttered Victorian assemblages adorned with kitschy Americana.

From the beginning it was recognized that the White House belonged to the people of the United States, and visitors were allowed virtually unlimited access to the mansion and its occupants. Security was almost nonexistent, as members of the public called upon the president, roamed the reception rooms, and darted into bedrooms to have a peek.

Receptions, parties, dinners, teas, dances, concerts, weddings, funerals, Cabinet meetings, and levees—formal gatherings designed to allow people of prominence an opportunity to meet the president—were held in the White House in the earliest administrations, and such events have continued to this day. Hundreds of ordinary citizens jammed through the White House doors for occasions like Andrew Jackson's inauguration celebration and Andrew Johnson's levees. Today, invitations to White House events are limited—but more than a million and a half tourists view the formal state rooms each year.

Like the country at whose political heart it stands, the White House has seen dramatic change. Yet, like the nation, the Executive Mansion and its occupants have retained familiar, comforting qualities, bringing the past into the present in a marvelous blend of valued tradition and spirited innovation.

Above: *Entertaining at the White House has reflected the differing styles of presidential families and their electorates. In the late 1850s, President James Buchanan aided by his elegant niece, Harriet Lane, received visitors in the East Room at a great public reception, with chandeliers glowing overhead, creating an aura of royal romance.*

GEORGE WASHINGTON

FIRST PRESIDENT
1789-1797
MARTHA D. CUSTIS WASHINGTON

GEORGE WASHINGTON was...
- the only president inaugurated in two cities—New York and Philadelphia.
- the only president unanimously elected, receiving all 69 electoral votes cast.
- the only president who did not live in Washington, D.C.
- the only president to be offered and to reject being made King.
- one of our wealthiest presidents, leaving an estate valued in 1799 at more than $500,000.

A MODEL LEADER

George Washington played an essential role in the founding of the United States of America. With his leadership on the battlefield, American forces triumphed over the British, thus securing American independence in 1783. With his steady hand and firm principles as first president of the new nation, he helped braid the multiple strands of the separate colonies and disparate interest groups into a single united national entity. Through all of his efforts, both physically dangerous and morally challenging, he enjoyed the continuous support of his wife Martha. Historians say the American presidency itself was modelled after the admirable personal traits of George Washington. Martha Washington also set high standards of grace and common sense which future presidential wives would emulate.

FAMILY LIFE

Young George's family were prosperous Virginia farmers, but his father died when the boy was eleven, and his mother was not easy to live with. As a youth, he struck out on his own as a surveyor and joined British American forces fighting in the French and Indian War. Notable at six-foot-two, lanky, engaging, and a splendid horseman, Washington moved up the military ladder to Lieutenant Colonel. In his early engagements with the French, his military strategies were considered less than brilliant. His bravery was astounding, however—in one battle he had two horses shot out from under him, and four bullets pierced his coat.

When his half-brother Lawrence died of tuberculosis, Washington inherited the fine plantation of Mount Vernon, to which he retired—temporarily—for sixteen years. A friend invited him to dinner and introduced him to a guest—the recently widowed and wealthy Martha Custis. Soon they were engaged, with George writing Martha that her life was "now inseparable" from his. Plighting his troth to Martha, however, did not prevent George from sending a love letter to his best friend's wife,

George Washington

In Office
Apr. 30, 1789-Mar. 3, 1797
Born Feb. 22, 1732,
Pope's Creek,
Westmoreland Co., Va.
Party: **Federalist**

Other Offices:
Member, Virginia House of Burgesses, 1758.
Member, First & Second Continental Congresses, 1774, 1775 .
Commander-in-Chief, Continental Army, 1775-83.
President, Constitutional Convention, 1787.
Lt.-Gen. and Commander-in-Chief, U.S. Army, 1798-99.

Marriage:
Martha Dandridge Custis Washington, 1759, married 40 yrs.

Presidential Acts:
Quelled Whiskey Rebellion.
Initiated building federal capital city.
Negotiated key treaties with Britain and Spain.
Established strong financial system, aided by Alexander Hamilton.

Died age 67, Dec. 14, 1799, Mt. Vernon, Va.

Left: George Washington's leadership inspired American rebels to triumph against the British in the Revolutionary War. In one of his decisive victories, he led his troops across the icy Delaware River to attack the enemy at Trenton, New Jersey. This heroic image of Washington crossing the Delaware (originally painted by Emanuel Leutze, copied by Eastman Johnson) has itself become part of the proud American tradition.

Sally Fairfax, two months later, declaring his secret affection for her—most probably never consummated. Young Washington did have a reputation as a flirt.

Mrs. Custis and Colonel Washington were married at Mount Vernon. Martha was lovely in yellow brocade, her hair powdered and looped with pearls. With the marriage, Martha added 17,000 acres to George's 5,000 and 300 slaves to his 49, as well as a Williamsburg town house and two children by her deceased husband, the indolent John and sickly Martha (Patsy), who died at seventeen. George and Martha had no children together, but Martha's grandchildren came to live with them in later years. The couple cooperated in successfully managing Mount Vernon. Although romance was perhaps not the primary factor which brought them together initially, the forty-year marriage proved to be extremely happy.

THE REVOLUTION

Washington took an active part in the incipient revolution, and in 1775 was elected commander-in-chief of a proposed Continental Army to fight for independence. Washington responded, "Though I am truly sensible of the higher honor done me in this appointment, yet I feel great distress for a consciousness that my abilities and military experience may not be equal to the extensive and important trust." Despite his self-doubts, Washington led his under-equipped, ill-paid and undertrained troops through years of miserable combat, coping with extreme heat and cold, to final victory over the British. Washington's brilliant leadership was essential to the success of the Revolution.

The bitter hardship of the 1777-78 winter encampment at Valley Forge was made slightly less intolerable by the fact that Martha Washington came to share rustic quarters with her husband,

Above: A week before his inauguration as the new nation's first president, Washington was trimphantly rowed across New York Bay to the foot of Wall Street in New York, the temporary federal capital. In honor of the thirteen colonies, thirteen white-uniformed pilots rowed, as cannons on ships and shore fired thirteen-gun salutes in exultant celebration.

Right: In a crucial test of federal strength, the Whisky Rebellion broke out in 1794 in western Pennsylvania against the federal excise tax on whisky. "Whisky Boys" raised havoc and tarred-and-feathered tax collectors. Washington mobilized thousands of troops to squelch the protest, thus affirming federal powers without firing a single shot.

Left: This portrait of Washington, as Commander-in-chief of the Continental Army, hangs at Mount Vernon.

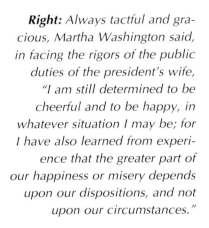

to cheerfully knit socks for the frostbitten troops, and to help soothe the sick. Martha and several other officers' wives spent each of eight winters during the Revolutionary War (combat ceased during the cold months) with the General and his men. "Whilst our husbands and brothers are examples of patriotism," she told them, "we must be patterns of industry."

SHAPING THE PRESIDENCY

After the war, Washington longed to return to a quiet life at Mount Vernon, but at age fifty-seven he was called to lead the American people's great experiment in democratic government. He set key precedents followed by all succeeding presidents. He named a Cabinet, considered himself the representative of all the people—not just of his own political party—, and shaped federal rights to tax, regulate currency and finance, and make treaties with foreign governments. He urged rejection of factionalism and foreign entanglements. He dismissed suggestions that he be made king, but he upheld the dignity of the presidency at all times, considering the office symbolic of the international prestige of the country.

Right: Always tactful and gracious, Martha Washington said, in facing the rigors of the public duties of the president's wife, "I am still determined to be cheerful and to be happy, in whatever situation I may be; for I have also learned from experience that the greater part of our happiness or misery depends upon our dispositions, and not upon our circumstances."

Martha D. Custis Washington

Born Jun. 21, 1731, New Kent County, VA
Children: **4 by first husband (2 died in infancy), none by Washington**

Accomplishments:
Managed Mount Vernon, increasing the prosperity of the huge estate, freeing her husband to lead the nation.

Died age 70, May 22, 1802, Mt. Vernon, Va.

Lady Washington, as she was known, arrived in New York a month after the inauguration and was amazed to be greeted by cheering crowds and the roars of cannons. In New York, and after 1790 when the government temporarily moved to Philadelphia, Martha held weekly drawing-room gatherings so guests could meet her and the president. Weekly official dinners were famous for both delicious food and long silences—neither George nor Martha were masters of small talk. She was, however, greatly admired for her tact, unassuming manners and sweetness.

After two terms, Washington retired to Mount Vernon, where he occupied himself with "rural amusement" for nearly three years. In 1799, an afternoon chill developed into serious illness, and he died quietly at home, his family at his bedside. Martha assured their personal privacy by burning their letters and lived until 1802, a respected great lady.

George Washington was eulogized by Thomas Jefferson, who wrote, "Never did nature and fortune combine more perfectly to make a man great, and to place him in...an everlasting remembrance." At Washington's funeral, his friend General Henry Lee declared, "First in war, first in peace, first in the hearts of his countrymen." Washington had left his mark forever on the presidency and his country.

Above: Plans for the federal capital are examined by General Washington, Martha, and two grandchildren, George Washington Parke Custis and Eleanor Parke Custis, in a family gathering painted by Edward Savage. The capital city was still under construction when Washington died.

Right: Known as "His Rotundity" behind his back, John Adams used his great powers of intellect and diplomacy to save the new nation from sure defeat in a threatened war with France. Often personally vain, he was sentimental and romantic with his wife, whom he valued as his true partner in life.

John Adams

In Office:
Mar. 4, 1797-Mar. 3, 1801
Born Oct. 30, 1735,
Braintree (now Quincy), Mass.
Party: Federalist

Other Offices:
Member, Mass. legislature,
1768, revolutionary congress,
1774, and Constitutional
Conventions, 1779 and 1820.
Member, First & Second
Continental Congresses,
1774, 1775.
Commissioner to France, 1778.
Minister to the Netherlands,
1780, to England, 1785-88.
Vice President, 1789-97.

Marriage:
Abigail Smith Adams, 1764,
married 54 yrs.

Presidential Acts:
Supported controversial
Naturalization, Alien, &
Sedition Acts, 1798.
Negotiated peace with France,
signed Treaty of Morfontaine,
1800.
Promoted construction of a
U.S. Navy.

Died age 90,
July 4, 1826,
Quincy, Mass.

JOHN ADAMS

SECOND PRESIDENT
1797-1801
ABIGAIL SMITH ADAMS

Harvard-educated and high-principled, John Adams succeeded the Father of His Country— a difficult thing to do. No swashbuckling hero, rotund Adams was strong in cognitive skills which he applied to preserving the new nation. His wife Abigail was intellectually and educationally his equal, virtually his partner in the presidency. Adams lacked charisma and tact and would probably never have been elected in a modern media-dominated campaign. It was fortunate, however, that his virtues were recognized by the Founding Fathers, for he saved the fledgling country from full-scale war with France.

FROM REVOLUTIONARY TO PRESIDENT

Of Massachusetts Puritan farmer ancestry, Adams became a teacher and lawyer after college. The orations of attorney James Otis and the patriotic rabble-rousing of his cousin Sam Adams sparked in John Adams the passionate desire to escape the injustice of British rule.

Protests against the Stamp Act, the Boston Massacre, and the Boston Tea Party were pivotal events for Adams. He helped draw up the Declaration of Independence and, with Benjamin Franklin and John Jay, negotiated the 1783 Treaty of Paris, in which Britain formally acknowledged the independence of the United States.

In office, Adams wrangled with Alexander Hamilton and Thomas Jefferson and lost popularity over his support of the Naturalization, Alien, and Sedition Acts, under which political opponents of the administration were imprisoned and deported.

Crisis with revolutionary France was the principal issue of Adams's single term. French harassment of American ships and demands for payoffs led to a national passion to avenge the insult. But clear-thinking Adams knew that war could ruin the country, and he skillfully negotiated a treaty establishing good relations with France.

NO ORDINARY WIFE

Abigail Adams was well-read and constantly offered Adams her political opinions. A minister's daughter, she brought out Adams's tender side, and their fifty-four-year marriage was an indivisible partnership of heart and mind. During his long periods away on political and diplomatic business, she raised their five children (one died young), managed their farm, and wrote him hundreds of letters. Her letters provide wonderful insights into the social history of the time. The power of her advice to her husband was well-known.

Abigail was an outspoken advocate of women's rights and believed the wife of the president ought to use her powerful position to do good—a notion which became part of the role.

The Adams family was the first to occupy the new White House, still woefully incomplete and set in isolated splendor amid a swampy landscape. Abigail had to dry laundry in the "audience room," now known as the East Room. Newly arrived in Washington, Abigail was shocked to see slaves laboring while their owners stood idle.

Defeated for reelection by his vice president, Jefferson, Adams lived decades after his term—long enough to see his son John Quincy elected president. Abigail had died earlier—brilliant, dissatisfied with limitations on females, wife of a president, mother of a president—and yet she could not even vote. John Adams died on July 4, 1826—the fiftieth anniversary of the signing of the Declaration of Independence. Adams's last words were "Jefferson still survives," but actually, Jefferson had died several hours earlier upon the same day.

Below:
Abigail Adams spoke out for women in an era when it was unthinkable that women might one day have the vote. When the Constitution was being drafted, she admonished her husband, "I desire you would remember the ladies and be more generous and favorable to them than your ancestors. Do not push such unlimited power into the hands of husbands. Remember, all men would be tyrants if they could."

Abigail Smith Adams

Born Nov. 11, 1744, Weymouth, Mass.
Children: **3 sons, 2 daughters**

Accomplishments:
**Managed family, household, & farm during husband's long absences.
Advocated feminist principles, opposed slavery.
Considered "doing good" essential to role of president's wife.**

Died age 73, Oct. 28, 1818, Quincy, Mass.

Left: Hostilities with Revolutionary France plagued the young United States, including numerous naval battles. Here the French ship L'Insurgente surrenders to the U.S.S. Constitution ("Old Ironsides") in 1799. Adams's greatest triumph was avoiding full-scale war with France.

THOMAS JEFFERSON

THIRD PRESIDENT
1801-1809

On the Jefferson Memorial in Washington, D.C. is carved this quotation from the Third President: "I have sworn upon the altar of God, eternal hostility against every form of tyranny over the mind of man."

Thomas Jefferson considered his two terms as president among his less important accomplishments. A well-to-do Virginia planter, he was also a statesman and politician, writer, lawyer, architect, naturalist, musician, linguist, classicist, philosopher, scientist, inventor, and geographer. His interests ranged from pondering the essential relationships among God, government, and humankind to studying Gaelic and introducing the moldboard plow to farmers.

Jefferson's greatest achievement was drafting the Declaration of Independence, clearly affirming the unassailability of human liberty. For Jefferson—influenced by English philosopher John Locke—human rights were granted by God and could not be taken away by tyrannical governments. If a government ceased to provide life, liberty, and the pursuit of happiness for its people, it was the duty of people to rebel against it and form another. Jefferson's soaring phrases declaring the inherent worth of the common man inspired and shaped thought in America and throughout the world from his time to the present.

The American democracy rests on Jeffersonian ideals: the separation of church and state, universal suffrage, public education, humane objectives in the criminal code. He urged the abolition of slavery but freed only a handful of his two hundred slaves during his lifetime. Enlightened

Thomas Jefferson

In Office
Mar. 4, 1801-Mar. 3, 1809
Born
Apr. 13, 1743, Shadwell, Va.
Party: **Democratic-Republican**

Other Offices:
Member, Virginia House of Burgesses, 1769-74
Member, Continental Congress, 1775, 1776, Chairman, Committee to draft the Declaration of Independence
Governor of Virginia, 1779-81
Minister to France, 1784-89
Secretary of State, 1789-93
Vice President, 1797-1801
Rector, University of Virginia, 1819

Marriage:
Martha Wayles Skelton Jefferson, 1772, married 10 yrs.
Children by Jefferson: 5 daughters, 1 son.
(Born 1748, died 1782)

Presidential Acts:
Purchased Louisiana Territory from France for $16 million.
Initiated Lewis & Clark Expedition, 1804-06.
Fought successful war against Tripoli, 1804-05.
Enforced embargo on American foreign shipping, 1807-09 to avoid entanglement in European war.
Faced *Chesapeake-Leopard* Affair (British attacked U.S. ship), prelude to War of 1812.

Died age 83, July 4, 1826, Charlottesville, Va.

Left: Martha Skelton Jefferson was a cheerful and musical partner for Jefferson—she played the piano-forte, while he played the violin. She bore many children, most of whom died. She herself died young, leaving Jefferson bereft. Committed to privacy, he removed all traces of her, and no authentic portrait survives. A later artistic recreation conveys a sense of how she might have appeared.

Right: The eyes of a philosopher shine from this portrait of Thomas Jefferson by Gilbert Stuart. Jefferson was one of the greatest intellects America has ever produced. His brilliant thinking and dedication to human liberty have influenced the lives of countless millions around the globe.

HOME AND FAMILY

Jefferson was one of ten children born to an aristocratic Virginia tobacco plantation owner and his well-born wife. He graduated from the College of William and Mary and prospered as a lawyer. Over six feet, red-haired, shy, and slender, he successfully courted a young widow, Martha Wayles Skelton, whose young husband and little son had died. They were married on New Year's Day in 1772, and Jefferson took his bride through the snowdrifts to his plantation home at Monticello. Their early days were filled with affection and laughter, and Martha (or Patty, as he called her) gave birth to six children in ten years. Of these but two lived to maturity, and only one, daughter Martha (Patsy) lived past twenty-five.

Merry, outgoing Martha never stepped outside Virginia. Her father, a wealthy English immigrant, married twice and also had a half-white slave woman as a mistress, by whom he fathered a daughter named Sally Hemings. When her father died, Martha's large inheritance doubled the Jefferson wealth. Along with other slaves, Sally came to Monticello.

Martha did not share her husband's commitment to the Revolution. When Jefferson was governor of Virginia, Martha enjoyed gala official life in Williamsburg but brushed aside a request from Lady Washington to lead her state's drive for the soldier-relief program.

Jefferson spearheaded not only the writing of the Declaration of Independence but also wrote other important protests against tyranny. In Virginia, in 1779, he introduced the Act for Establishing Religious Freedom, a classic bill guaranteeing freedom of religion without state intervention.

With constant childbearing, Martha's health failed, and despite Jefferson's attentive nursing, she died in 1782 at age thirty-three. Jefferson was grief-stricken and deeply depressed for several months. He never remarried, although he apparently had a long-time liaison with his wife's half-sister Sally, resulting in five children, of whom four survived to adulthood.

THE PRESIDENCY AND BEYOND

Tearing himself away from his beloved Monticello, Jefferson carried out diplomatic assignments in Europe and joined Washington's and Adams's administrations. He worked against the repressive Alien and Sedition Acts and suffered through a vicious election campaign for the presidency.

At fifty-seven, Jefferson was the first Chief Executive inaugurated in Washington. His first major foreign crisis involved Barbary Coast pirates raiding American ships; the offenders

Left: Politics were rough in Jefferson's time. Though considered today one of America's greatest leaders, when he ran for president in 1800 he was viciously attacked as a drunkard, the father of numerous mixed-race children, and an atheist. Here a Federalist political cartoon shows Jefferson attempting to pull down the federal government assisted by of his "old friend," the Devil.

Left: The Jeffersons resided at Monticello, the thirty-five-room home Jefferson designed and spent years expanding. Built on a hilltop near Charlottesville, Virginia, the red brick mansion's name means "little mountain." The building incorporates elements from classical structures in Italy and France and contains several Jefferson inventions, including a dumb-waiter and calendar clock. Thousands visit the home each year.

The United States in 1803

Above: *Purchasing the Louisiana Territory from France was one of the most important events in Jefferson's presidency. As this 1803 map shows, the new territory, stretching from the Mississippi River to the Continental Divide, essentially doubled the size of the United States—for a mere $16 million.*

Right: *A statue of Thomas Jefferson stands proudly at the University of Virginia, which he founded after his presidency. Jefferson designed the buildings, organized the curriculum, hired the faculty, and selected the library books. His design for the Rotunda, shown here, was based on the Pantheon in Rome, achieving a more graceful structure than the original.*

were vigorously squelched. But a much more important event took place at home—the purchase of the Louisiana Territory, doubling the size of the United States. Anticipating further westward expansion, Jefferson sent Lewis and Clark on their pioneering exploration of western lands.

Jefferson disliked the pseudo-royal pomp of the previous presidents and brought an informal atmosphere to the White House. He began the practice of having guests shake hands with the president, instead of bowing. Always interested in architecture, he developed ideas for the addition of terraces and a portico to the White House. He depended upon his daughter Patsy to preside over entertainments. Sophisticated and fluent in several languages, she was an adept hostess. She gave birth to a son there—the first child born in the White House. However, she had her own household to run, so official duties were often performed by Dolley Madison, wife of Secretary of State James Madison. Menus included European as well as American delicacies.

Jefferson easily won reelection, but during his second term, he became ensnared in an unpopular embargo on all U.S. trade with foreign lands, an attempt to prevent British and French harassment of U.S. ships. Congress made it illegal to import slaves, pleasing Jefferson, but he was ready to retire.

His last seventeen years were spent designing and establishing the University of Virginia, experimenting with rice growing making the U.S. a major producer, indulging in numerous other investigations, and writing on a vast range of subjects. He thoroughly followed his admonition to others, "Determine never to be idle....It is wonderful how much may be done if we are always doing." He died, as Adams did, on July 4, 1826, the fiftieth anniversary of the signing of his great creation, the Declaration of Independence.

JAMES MADISON

FOURTH PRESIDENT
1809-1817
DOLLEY TODD MADISON

James Madison was one of the small group of activist intellectuals who came of age during the American Revolution and guided the new nation for its first several decades. Unlike the tall, impressive Washington and Jefferson, Madison was short and underweight, but his bright mind illuminates his country to this day, for he was the Father of the Constitution.

Rather bookish and soft-spoken, Madison's best social asset was his wife Dolley, gregarious and charming to a degree still legendary in American history. While he was immersed in serious words and politics, she brought joy to the national scene and became possibly the country's most popular presidential wife.

STRUGGLE FOR FREEDOM

The oldest of twelve children of a prosperous Virginia planter, Madison studied at Princeton, where he learned notions of religious tolerance and gained an international outlook. He zealously tried to eliminate sleep so he could study longer but collapsed and spent two lonely years recuperating at home. Physically unfit for military service in the Revolution, he shouldered the burdens of statesmanship at the state and national levels, intelligently combining political science and law with a strong practical sense.

Madison met Jefferson in Virginia's first legislative assembly in 1776, and they began a lifelong friendship and constructive political partnership. While Jefferson was away in France, Madison successfully continued the struggle Jefferson had begun for separation of church and state in Virginia, opposing state support for teachers of the Christian religion. Upon passage of the religious freedom bill, Madison happily wrote to Jefferson that thus in Virginia, "was extinguished forever the ambitious hope of making laws for the human mind."

At the 1787 Constitutional Convention, thirty-six-year-old Madison took the leading role. Fully comprehending the problems of federalism, he contrived the system of checks and balances and solved the sticky problem of the composition of the legislature. His speeches and

---

James Madison

In Office
Mar. 4, 1809-Mar. 3, 1817
Born Mar. 16, 1751,
Port Conway, Va.
Party: Democratic-Republican

Other Offices:
Member, Virginia Legislature,
1776-77, 1784-86.
Member, Continental Congress,
1780-83, 1786-88.
Member & Chief Recorder,
Constitutional Convention,
1787.
U.S. Congressman, 1789-97.
Secretary of State, 1801-9.
Rector, University of Virginia,
1826.

Marriage:
Dolley Dandridge Payne Todd
Madison, 1794, married 41 yrs.

Presidential Acts:
Commander-in-Chief during
War of 1812.
Approved crushing of Indian
resistance at Tippecanoe.
Annexed Spanish West Florida.
Reestablished national bank.

Died age 85, Jun. 28, 1836,
Montpelier, Va.

Right: *During the War of 1812, Lieutenant Oliver Hazard Perry won a crucial victory over the British at the 1813 Battle of Lake Erie. "We have met the enemy and they are ours," he declared. Perry's ship flew a flag bearing the motto, "Don't give up the ship!"—the dying words of Captain James Lawrence killed in an earlier naval engagement during the war.*

Left: *A brilliant thinker, James Madison shaped the Constitution, expressing great democratic concepts in an articulate document which would be the framework upon which the nation would depend for centuries.*

writings helped secure ratification, and he later led the fight for the Bill of Rights.

"LADY PRESIDENTRESS"

Dolley Madison came not from an aristocratic background, but rather a penniless Quaker household. Morally opposed to slavery, her father had freed his slaves and then, without laborers, found it impossible to run his farm, which he sold. The family, with nine children, struggled to survive in a small Philadelphia house. Despite her dull gray Quaker dress, Dolley shone as a beauty of fine character. She married John Todd, had two small boys, and was just moving out of poverty when tragedy struck. In 1793, a yellow fever epidemic decimated the city, and Dolley lost her husband, little son, and many relatives.

Dolley's mother ran a rooming house, and there Dolley met Aaron Burr, who introduced her to the shy Congressman Madison, one of the half-dozen great men of the day. Magnetic Dolley won Madison's heart and finally consented to marry him in 1794.

Dolley's zest and gaiety made up for her sketchy education, and she became one of the great hostesses of Philadelphia while it was the national capital, and also presided at Montpelier, Madison's huge plantation. Later, in Washington, while Madison was Jefferson's Secretary of State, Dolley honed her social skills as occasional White House hostess for the widowed president.

Jefferson chose Madison to succeed him as President. "Lady Presidentress" Dolley organized the first inaugural ball and escalated her entertainments, dazzling Washington with her formal state dinners and splendid parties. She was the first to serve ice cream in the mansion. She decorated the house with fine furniture and damask and appeared dressed in elegant finery topped with turbans adorned with bird-of-paradise plumes. Her sister Lucy's wedding to a Supreme Court justice was the first in the White House. Women constantly asked her advice and approval, and in her time, she became the single greatest influence on women.

THE WAR OF 1812

Madison faced insoluble problems created by French and British hostilities during the European Napoleonic Wars. American ships were being attacked, and most irritating, the British were seizing cargoes and kidnaping American seamen. All schemes to halt these insults failed.

Congressional "War Hawks" and other interests pressured the president to ask Congress to declare war on Britain, commencing the War of 1812. This ill-advised struggle led to a series of intense battles with no permanent territorial gain on either side. The 1814 bombardment of Ft. McHenry by the British inspired Francis Scott Key to compose the song that would become the national anthem. Andrew Jackson emerged as the hero of the battle for New Orleans.

During the war, 14,000 British soldiers surged into Washington, D.C., burning and pillaging as they went. While the president was out assaying the situation and then running for his life,

Dolley Madison, writing to her sister from the White House, Aug. 24, 1814, three o'clock, as British invaders marched on the capital, intent on destruction:

Will you believe it, my sister, we have had a battle...near Bladensburg [Md.], and I am still here within sound of the cannon! Mr. Madison comes not; may God protect him! Two messengers, covered with dust, come to bid me fly; but I wait for him....At this late hour a wagon has been procured...I insist on waiting until the large picture of General Washington is secured....I have ordered the frame to be broken and the canvas taken out; it is done, and the precious portrait placed in the hands of two gentlemen of New York for safe-keeping. And now, dear sister, I must leave this house....where I shall be tomorrow, I cannot tell!

courageous Dolley packed valuable documents and silver into a wagon and tore out of the White House just in time. The invaders ate still-warm food in the mansion and then torched it, leaving only a smoldering shell.

Amazingly, the war was followed by an upsurge of nationalism, and Madison emerged with enhanced prestige. In temporary quarters, Dolley gave more parties, and the White House was ultimately rebuilt. The couple retired to Montpelier for nineteen years, where Madison became a gentleman farmer and succeeded Jefferson as head of the University of Virginia. Energetic Dolley outlived him and returned to Washington to become the doyenne of society for another decade. She played matchmaker for widower President Van Buren's son, introducing him to her cousin, who then served as White House hostess, guided by Dolley's expert advice. Much beloved at her death, Dolley was mourned by thousands at an elaborate funeral. President Zachary Taylor declared, "She will never be forgotten, because she was truly our First Lady for a half-century."

Dolley D. P. Todd Madison

Born May 20, 1768, Guilford County, N.C.
Children: 2 sons by first husband (1 died in infancy), none by Madison

Accomplishments:
Served as White House hostess for Jefferson & Madison. Set trends in fashion and entertaining. Responsible for the rescue of valuable items from the White House before its burning by the British. Advised & encouraged succeeding First Ladies.

Died at 81, Jul. 12, 1849, Montpelier, Va.

Left: *Dolley Madison reigned as the most admired hostess of Washington society not only during her husband's presidency but for years thereafter. Cheerful and lively, as shown in this 1804 Gilbert Stuart portrait, she brought a unique charm to the White House, where she held many splendid entertainments and benevolently outshone all other women in the new capital city.*

Right: James Monroe rose from teen-aged soldier in Washington's army to the presidency. He was the last of the dynasty of Virginia-born presidents, and the last of the great eighteenth-century leaders to become Chief Executive.

James Monroe

In Office
Mar. 4, 1817-Mar. 3, 1825
Born Apr. 28, 1758,
Westmoreland Co., Va.
Party: **Democratic-Republican**

Other Offices:
Major, Continental Army,
1775-80.
Virginia Military Commissioner,
1780.
Member, Virginia House of
Delegates, 1782.
Member, Continental Congress,
1783-06.
Virginia Assemblyman,
1786, 1810.
U.S. Senator, 1790-94.
Minister to France, 1794-96.
Governor of Virginia,
1799-1803, 1811.
Minister to France, England,
1803.
Mission to Spain, England,
1804-06.
Secretary of State, 1811-17.
Secretary of War, 1814.
Regent, University of Virginia,
1826.

Marriage:
Elizabeth Kortright Monroe,
1786, married 44 yrs.

Presidential Acts:
Articulated Monroe Doctrine
warning against European
encroachment in the Americas.
Authorized Seminole War,
1817.
Purchased Florida from Spain
for $5 million, 1819.
Arranged Missouri Compromise.

Died age 73, Jul. 4, 1831,
New York, N.Y.

JAMES MONROE

FIFTH PRESIDENT
1817-1825
ELIZABETH
KORTRIGHT
MONROE

James Monroe came to the presidency with fifty years of experience in public service behind him. He glided naturally into his new role and completed two relatively uneventful terms. His wife Elizabeth seemed to move into her new role less gracefully than he did, and her stiff manner offended citizens and foreign diplomats alike.

Monroe was not of the aristocracy, and his father died when he was young. He walked miles to a rural school in the company of another boy, John Marshall, future Supreme Court Chief Justice. Monroe's uncle, a wealthy judge, took him under his wing, paid for his education at William and Mary, and later introduced him to Thomas Jefferson, who became his patron.

SERVICE ABROAD

Teen-aged Monroe fought in Washington's army, was wounded at Trenton, and received a commendation from the General himself. Jefferson, Governor at the time, taught Monroe law. Monroe soon began a political career, and Washington sent him as Minister to the French Republic.

Monroe had married Elizabeth Kortright, a highly respectable young woman from a mercantile New York family. They had two daughters and a little son—the boy died at three while Monroe was Governor of Virginia. Monroe's family accompanied him to Paris, where they enjoyed a luxurious life style. Little Eliza attended school with Napoleon's stepdaughter, and she and her mother affected French manners and fashion.

In Paris, Elizabeth performed the single most significant act for which she is known. She learned that Madame Lafayette, wife of the Marquis de Lafayette, America's friend, was imprisoned by the revolutionary government. Elizabeth ostentatiously drove to the prison in a carriage and boldly asked to see the prisoner. Madame Lafayette tearfully threw herself at Elizabeth Monroe's feet, declaring that she was about to be executed. Indeed, Mrs. Monroe's visit saved Madame Lafayette from the guillotine, since the French were reminded how popular Lafayette was in the United States and did not wish to offend the young republic. Madame Lafayette was released. Later, Monroe secured the release of Thomas Paine from a French prison.

THE ERA OF GOOD FEELING

Monroe was not a great success as a diplomat but earned admiration as a splendid administrator as Madison's Secretary of War. After Madison's retirement, Monroe was virtually a shoo-in for two terms as president, during what was called the "Era of Good Feeling." He went on a thirteen-state good-will tour and met with cheering crowds everywhere. The question of slavery was becoming a serious matter, and like many of the southern elite, Monroe opposed slavery even though he owned slaves. He supported the return of American slaves to the African country of Liberia; the capital of that country is named Monrovia in his honor. At home, Monroe tried to balance the numbers of slave and free states through the Missouri Compromise measure. During his time in office, the U.S. grew from fifteen to twenty-four states.

The Monroe Doctrine was announced to Congress in 1823—a warning to would-be European imperialists to keep out of the Western Hemisphere which would reverberate for many generations. During Monroe's time, the Russians were dissuaded from expanding their Alaskan territories, and Spain was induced to sell all of Florida to the United States.

A FORMAL HOSTESS

In 1817, the Monroes moved into the newly-renovated White House, its scorched walls and interior rebuilt anew. The barren rooms were furnished with furniture they had brought with them from France—including a chair once owned by Marie Antoinette—as well as costly new imports from Paris. Elizabeth opened the mansion for the usual New Year's reception in 1818, and with roaring fires in the fireplaces and candles glittering, the event was a great success. Elizabeth and her daughters stood regally upon a dais, nodding and smiling at the visitors the President handed past. For some, however, the furnishings, the women's high Empire style gowns, and the stiff etiquette were all too French, a haughty contrast with Dolley Madison's unaffected American style.

Unfortunately, after Dolley's fantastic social popularity, Elizabeth seemed cold and aloof. Elizabeth let it be known that she would essentially make no social calls and would seldom receive callers. Wives of the diplomatic corps were so offended, Monroe had to call a special cabinet meeting to discuss the issue. For a time, Washington women boycotted the few events she did organize. Although attendance eventually increased, the White House was a fairly dull place for eight years. Even the wedding of Monroe's youngest daughter Maria was strictly private, and gifts from officials were coldly discouraged.

Many felt that Elizabeth had a "queen" complex, and snobbery was undoubtedly involved. However, unknown to outsiders, Elizabeth apparently suffered from epileptic seizures and was afraid to embarrass herself. Elizabeth could have avoided much criticism if she had simply pleaded ill health.

For five years after retirement, the Monroes enjoyed living at Oak Hill, their grand Virginia country home. After Elizabeth's death, Monroe sold Oak Hill and moved to New York to reside with his daughter's family. He died on July 4, 1831, the third president to pass away on the anniversary of the nation's birth.

Below: As the president's wife, Elizabeth Monroe brought French manners to the White House—and endured accusations that she was too formal and aloof for American tastes. Actually, she suffered from an illness that she tried to conceal by minimizing social contacts.

Left: Russians hunted for sea mammals in the Arctic—and hoped to expand the Czar's Alaskan territories as far south as Oregon. Monroe reacted sharply to such efforts, setting forth his famous Monroe Doctrine (actually written by John Quincy Adams), declaring all independent nations of the Western Hemisphere off limits for European interference or colonization.

Elizabeth Kortright Monroe

Born Jun. 30, 1768, New York, N.Y.
Children: **2 daughters, 1 son**

Accomplishments:
**Saved Madame Lafayette from execution.
Was hostess & a valuable social asset for her husband during his missions abroad.
Known in Europe as "la belle Americaine."
Regarded less favorably as First Lady.**

Died age 62, Sept. 23, 1830, Oak Hill, Va.

Right: *John Quincy Adams was inaugurated president nearly a quarter century after his father stepped down as chief executive, bringing with him skills he learned as his father's assistant. His progressive visions for the country's future were thwarted during his administration but eventually took shape as key national institutions.*

John Quincy Adams

In Office:
Mar. 4, 1825-Mar. 3, 1829
Born July 11, 1767,
Braintree (now Quincy), Mass.
Party: Democratic-Republican

Other Offices:
Secretary to Minister to Russia, 1781.
Secretary to John Adams, Minister to Great Britain, 1785.
Minister to the Netherlands, Portugal, Prussia, 1794-97.
Massachusetts State Senator, 1802.
U.S. Senator, 1803-8.
Minister to Russia, 1809-14.
Negotiator, Treaty of Ghent, 1814.
Minister to England, 1815-17.
Secretary of State, 1817-25.
U.S. Congressman, 1831-48.

Died age 77, May 14, 1852.

Marriage:
Louisa Catherine Johnson Adams, 1797, married 50 yrs.

Presidential Acts:
Advocated federal support for numerous key improvements in national infrastructure.
Supported justice for American Indians and slaves.

Died age 80,
Feb. 23, 1848,
Washington, D.C.

JOHN QUINCY ADAMS

SIXTH PRESIDENT
1825-1829

LOUISA C. JOHNSON ADAMS

John Quincy Adams, son of the Second President, was brilliant, experienced, and accomplished, yet his personal manner was so annoying he frequently offended his wife, fellow statesmen, and ordinary voters. He was fortunate to have the help of his talented wife Louisa during his long and challenging career.

As a teenager, he stood at his father's side at the signing of the Treaty of Paris, formalizing American independence. Before he entered Harvard, he had already been secretary to the ministers to Russia and Great Britain. By age thirty, he had himself been minister to three countries.

MARRIAGE AND DIPLOMACY

While in England, he met London-born Louisa, the intelligent and musical daughter of a Maryland diplomat; she had been finely educated in Britain and France. They married in

Right: Chief negotiator of the Treaty of Ghent, ending the War of 1812, black-garbed John Quincy Adams steps forward to shake the hand of Lord Gambier, the British representative, on Christmas Eve, 1814. The treaty signalled the beginning of a new era in which Great Britain and the United States would settle all disputes peacefully.

London and resided in The Hague and Berlin during Adams' diplomatic missions there. Later, they spent six years in St. Petersburg. While Adams was away negotiating the end to the War of 1812, Louisa courageously travelled with her eight-year-old son for forty days in a horse-drawn coach across a thousand snowy miles from Russia to Paris, while Napoleon was on the march. Her hair-raising adventures scarcely impressed her husband, who was not particularly sympathetic to women's feelings.

Adams thought that women were rightly subordinate to men and once said that mental abilities were "unbecoming in a female." This was somewhat surprising, since his mother, Abigail Adams, was an early advocate of equal treatment for men and women. The couple often disagreed on decision-making in household matters. Louisa was ill through numerous pregnancies and miscarriages, and her baby daughter died, leaving her with three sons.

Monroe selected Adams as his Secretary of State—a very wise move, since Adams's skills at the job were superb. It was Adams who wrote the passage known as the Monroe Doctrine, and it was Adams's firmness that convinced the Russians not to try to take over the Pacific Northwest. During the Monroe administration, Louisa was the leading Washington hostess; her entertainments were much more popular than Mrs. Monroe's. She held the grandest party of the decade—a lavish ball for Andrew Jackson on the ninth anniversary of his victory over the British at the Battle of New Orleans.

UNFULFILLED GOALS

During the 1824 election, Jackson won the popular vote over Adams and other candidates, but noone won a majority of the electoral votes. The election was thrown into the House of Representatives, which chose Adams. Rancorous charges stung the new administration.

In this time of peace, Adams had a progressive vision for the country—including an interstate network of roads and canals, a Department of the Interior, mapping expeditions, a naval academy, and government aid to education. During Adams's term, Congress rejected these proposals—although, of course, all eventually became reality. Adams pleaded for Western territory to be provided for Indians, but the more popular attitude was Jackson's approach—a mixture of eviction and extermination.

Louisa was a gracious and cultured hostess at the White House, but she suffered deep depression there. The marriage had always been troubled, but it reached its low point in the echoing halls of the mansion. In 1829, the suicide of their reprobate eldest son was a severe blow, mitigated only by the joys of their two living sons and grandchildren.

Adams felt it beneath his ethics to campaign, so he lost his reelection bid badly. Soon, however, he was elected a Massachusetts representative to Congress—the only former president ever to serve in that capacity. In Congress he was known as "Old Man Eloquent," and there he spent his greatest seventeen years. This was also the best period for the Adams' marriage. Together, the couple worked against slavery, and both broadened their ideas on equality of the sexes. The fifty-year-partnership ended on a note of harmony and mutual respect.

Above: Louisa Adams was the only First Lady born outside the United States, the talented daughter of American parents living in London. Her spirit of independence helped her successfully struggle with depression and her husband's arrogance. A ball she held in honor of Andrew Jackson was acclaimed the grandest social event of the 1820s.

ANDREW JACKSON

SEVENTH PRESIDENT
1829-1837

ANDREW JACKSON was the first president...
- born in a log cabin.
- born west of the Allegheny Mountains.
- to marry a divorced woman.
- to have been nominated by a national nominating convention.
- to ride on a railroad train while in office.

Americans loved Andrew Jackson when he ran for office and still loved him eight years later when he stepped down. With Jackson as president, the intellectual elite of the East were replaced by a log-cabin-born, corncob-pipe-smoking chief executive. Short on philosophical ponderings, Jackson was long on gut-reactions. For the growing middle class, he embodied the American dream.

Born poor in the Carolina woods, he began his military career at age thirteen as a mounted orderly in the Revolutionary War. Captured, he defied a British officer's order to clean his boots, and the officer slashed him with a saber, leaving scars on his head and arm. With his parents both dead, Jackson became "the most roaring, rollicking, game-cocking, horse-racing, card-playing, mischievous fellow...the head of rowdies hereabouts...."

A DEVOTED COUPLE

He studied law and moved west to Tennessee, where he fell in love with delightful Rachel Robards, separated from a pathologically jealous husband. When they heard that Lewis Robards had obtained a divorce in Virginia, Jackson and Rachel married. Not until two years later did they learn that Robards had only *filed* for divorce, so technically Rachel was guilty of bigamy. With the divorce completed, Jackson and Rachel married again, and their long union was filled with tenderness.

The energetic backwoodsman went to Congress and then became a judge. Jackson challenged to a duel a man who alluded to Rachel's matrimonial record, and killed the offender. As major general in the U.S. Volunteers, he led a harsh campaign against the Creek Indians—a preview of his later cruel injustices against other Indian groups. Jackson wanted equality only for white men—he owned slaves and saw nothing wrong with it.

Devoted Rachel, an unsophisticated country woman, wanted her husband to spend more time at their Tennessee home, The Hermitage, where she was raising adopted and foster children and

Above: Helping themselves to chunks of a huge cheese are guests at a White House public reception. The 1,400-pound cheese was among many gifts received by President Jackson. True to his reputation as The People's President, he offered it to the voters who put him in office.

running the farm. For her, the "public place" held but "strife and empty honors."

But Jackson was drawn by the roar of the crowds to run for President. Famed for his victory at New Orleans, he won the election handily. But he and Rachel were stunned by his opponents' malicious campaign literature questioning the right of "a convicted adultress and her paramour husband" to be placed in the highest offices of the land. Overweight and distraught, Rachel died of a heart attack before Jackson could take the oath of office. The weeping widower cried he could never forgive the "vile wretches" who had destroyed his "dear saint."

MAN OF THE PEOPLE

In deep mourning, Jackson was inaugurated before huge crowds of people. Pale and dressed all in black, the ailing hero shook every offered hand in the crowd around him. The mob followed him to the White House, burst through the doors, and hurled itself on the refreshments. China was smashed, furniture was crushed, noses were bloodied, and women fainted. Jackson escaped through the back door.

His first presidential crisis was the matter of Peggy Eaton, the reputedly promiscuous wife of the Secretary of War. While Washington society snubbed her, Jackson gallantly defended her, probably because of his beloved Rachel's sufferings from slander. Secretary of State Martin Van Buren found a gentlemanly way for Eaton to resign quietly and thus earned for himself Jackson's support as his hand-picked successor.

Jackson's hostess was Emily Donelson, a niece married to a favorite nephew. Though only in her early twenties, she carried out family and official duties with tactful skill. Three of her children were born at the White House. Always frail, she died at twenty-eight from tuberculosis.

Jackson faced off against South Carolina secessionists protesting tariffs they disliked, declaring that the union must be preserved at all costs. His statements, "No state or states has a right to secede," and "Disunion by armed force is *treason*," were unhappy harbingers of the Civil War to come.

Jackson retired after two terms, second only to Washington in his influence on the Presidency. At The Hermitage, his chronic ailments and injuries finally caught up with him. As he lay dying, he said to his family and servants, "Oh, do not cry. Be good children, and we shall all meet in Heaven."

Right: Injustices to Native Americans and African Americans were a hallmark of the Jacksonian era. As European Americans of every level of society clamored for land and economic opportunity, Indians and slaves were harshly exploited, as at this slave auction. In 1831, an antislavery newspaper, The Liberator, began publication—giving voice to the growing abolitionist movement.

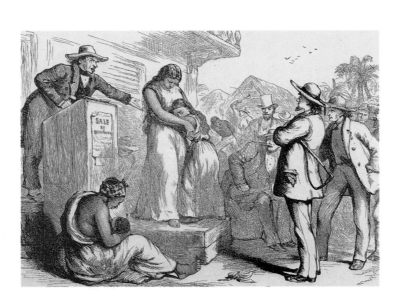

Right: Rachel Jackson wanted nothing more than a quiet home life, but undeserved scandalous accusations led to her sudden demise before she could become First Lady. Heartbroken, Jackson kept her portrait with him daily and at his bedside every night. Tradition holds that this was the very image he carried.

Right: Honest and immaculately groomed, Martin Van Buren worked his way up in politics through shrewd but friendly political maneuvers. This painting by Henry Inman depicts Van Buren as Governor of New York in 1829, with the Albany capitol behind him. His much-loved wife Hanna had passed away four years earlier.

Martin Van Buren

In Office
Mar. 4, 1837-Mar. 3, 1841
Born Dec. 5, 1782,
Kinderhook, N.Y.
Party: **Democratic;**
Free-Soil after 1848

Early Offices:
N.Y. State Senator, 1813-20
Attorney General, N.Y. State,
1815-19
U.S. Senator, 1821-28
Governor of N.Y., 1829
Secretary of State, 1829-31
Vice President, 1833-37

Marriage:
Hanna Hoes Van Buren, 1807,
married nearly 12 yrs.
Children: 4 sons.
(Born 1783, Died 1819)

Presidential Acts:
Faced the Panic of 1837
and Depression.
Advocated Independent
Treasury.
Defused British/Canadian-
American tension over U.S. ship
Caroline sunk while aiding
Canadian freedom fighters.
Arranged Canadian-US truce
over Canadians cutting timber
in Maine.

Died age 79, Jul. 24, 1862,
Kinderhook, N.Y.

MARTIN VAN BUREN

EIGHTH PRESIDENT
1837-1841
ANGELICA
SINGLETON
VAN BUREN

Martin Van Buren, America's first systematic national politician, made his way through the treacherous shoals of state and national politics for decades. His 1836 presidential campaign initials, O.K., from "Old Kinderhook" (his home town), were the origin of the expression that has been with us ever since. Within days of his inauguration, he faced the biggest economic crisis ever to threaten the young nation. He dealt forcefully with this and other serious matters without a wife at his side, as the mother of his four sons had died young.

Childhood sweethearts in a close-knit Dutch American community, Van Buren and his wife Hanna conversed in Dutch and were married not quite twelve years. A quiet, kind woman, she fell victim to tuberculosis at age thirty-five and is known only by her obituary, which read in part, "Modest and unassuming, possessing the most engaging simplicity of manners, her heart was the residence of every kind affection, and glowed with sympathy for the wants and sufferings of others....Humility was her crowning grace...." She exemplified the perfect woman of her time. Van Buren never remarried, despite meeting many eligible women in his progress from state legislator to the highest office in the land.

Van Buren's ardent work on Jackson's political campaigns earned him Jackson's approval as his heir apparent. Unfortunately, Jackson also bequeathed him a huge fiscal calamity, the Panic of 1837. A speculative boom in western lands, inadequately regulated by Jackson's administration, fed a bank panic that surged across the country and led to several years of general Depression. Van Buren responded with a creditable plan for an independent federal treasury—enacted finally in 1840.

PRESIDENTIAL HOUSEKEEPING

When Van Buren entered the White House, the mansion needed refurbishing, and the new president used a government appropriation along with his own money to freshen up the house.

New wallpaper was hung in all the state rooms, woodwork repainted, mahogany doors varnished, chandeliers restrung, and cushions installed. For the gracious oval room, designed as a chamber to receive callers formally, Van Buren selected new decorations for the room in tones of blue, thus establishing it in 1837 as the Blue Room, which it has remained ever since.

Like the presidents before him and several after him, Van Buren was personally responsible for engaging and paying the White House staff. The earliest presidents were provided only with the use of the edifice and one or two guards and perhaps a yardman. They had to supply their own household help, food, drink, horses, and coaches. The numerous official guests, callers, and univited freeloaders who appeared at White House meals and parties were fed out of the president's own pocket. Fortunately, Van Buren was a wealthy man—but he was still accused by political enemies of living like a king at public expense.

Left: Angelica Singleton Van Buren adorned the White House as hostess for her widowed father-in-law. Dolley Madison played matchmaker, introducing her distant cousin Angelica to the president's oldest son, Abraham. Her polished manners delighted some—and irritated others.

REGAL AIRS AND GRACES

After a time, social life at the White House was guided by a distant cousin of Dolley Madison's, Angelica Singleton Van Buren. Dolley had engineered Angelica's marriage to the president's son Abraham. Vivacious Angelica affected European sophistication and pretentious court manners. Angelica had visited Europe, and she put into practice something she had seen in the French and English courts. Angelica, along with her young women relatives and friends, would wear elaborate white gowns and flowers and arrange themselves in a living tableau to be viewed by guests. These pseudo-regal theatricals were considered absurd and even offensive by many White House visitors.

Although those who knew Van Buren personally invariably spoke well of him, his political enemies relentlessly exaggerated his "kingly" life style. In those troubled times, Van Buren sought reelection—not once, but twice—but did not win either time.

Left: The White House floats romantically above the banks of Tiber Creek in this etching dating from 1839 or 1840. Picturesque, yet emitting undesirable humidity and mosquitoes, the waterway was filled in some four decades later, becoming today's bustling Constitution Avenue.

Angelica Singleton Van Buren

(President's daughter-in-law)
Born 1816, Sumter District, S.C.

Marriage:
Abraham Van Buren
(President's eldest son)
November, 1838

Children:
3 sons, 1 daughter
(girl died in infancy)

Accomplishments:
Served as White House hostess after marriage. Praised for glittering entertainments and criticized for ostentatious behavior.

Died age 62, December 29, 1878, New York, N.Y.

Right: William Henry Harrison had the misfortune of becoming the first American president to die in office. He served the shortest term of any president in history—just one month. Harrison had a long and gallant career as a military leader and politician before the lure of the presidency pulled him out of retirement.

William Henry Harrison

In Office
Mar. 4, 1841–Apr. 4, 1841
Born Feb. 9, 1773, Berkeley,
Charles City County, Va.
Party: Whig

Early Offices:
Secretary of the Northwest
Territory, 1798-99
U.S. Congressman, 1799-1800,
1816-19
Territorial Governor of Indiana,
1801-13
Commander, U.S. forces, Battle
of Tippecanoe, 1811
Major General, War of 1812
U.S. Senator, 1825-28
Minister to Colombia, 1828-29

Marriage:
Anna Tuthill Symmes Harrison,
1795, married 45 yrs.

Presidential Acts: none

Died age 68, Apr. 4, 1841

Anna Symmes Harrison

Born Jul. 25, 1775,
Morristown, N.J.

Children: 6 sons, 4 daughters

Accomplishments:
Raised large family, active in
church and community life.
Served as hostess during
Harrison's term as Governor of
Indiana territory, but never
served as First Lady.

Died age 88, Feb. 25, 1864,
North Bend, Ohio

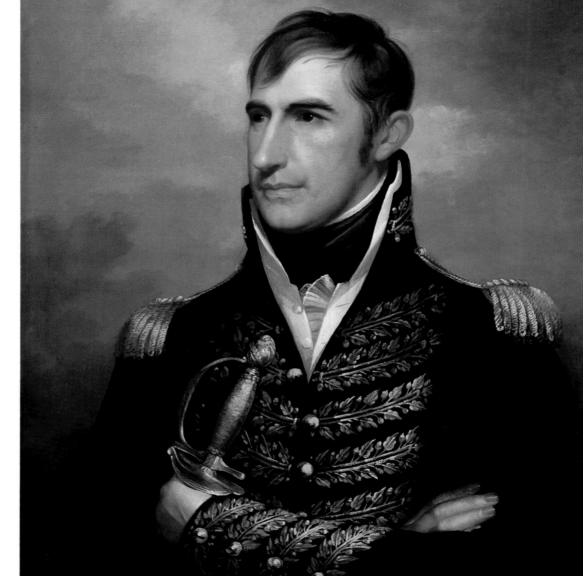

WILLIAM HENRY HARRISON

NINTH PRESIDENT
1841
ANNA T. SYMMES HARRISON

A Virginian by birth but a frontier fighter and farmer by occupation, William Henry Harrison brought patrician blood lines and personal courage to the presidency. Unfortunately, he caught a bad cold at his chilly inauguration which, in combination with ill-advised "treatments" by his physicians, killed him only one month after he took office. His wife Anna was still back in Ohio packing to leave for Washington when he died, and she never set foot in the White House.

Harrison's father, Benjamin Harrison, had been a signer of the Declaration of Independence. Young Harrison used his father's friendship with George Washington to obtain an ensign's commission in the army, and was soon fighting Indians in the Midwest. There he wooed Anna

Symmes, herself raised in Eastern society but transplanted to the frontier with her prosperous family.

MARRIAGE AND FAMILY

As independent as her husband, Anna defied her father and eloped with the dashing soldier who would father her ten children. A strong-minded homebody, she managed the ever-increasing family's home and education while her husband fought Chief Tecumseh at the 1811 Battle of Tippecanoe, near present-day Lafayette, Indiana, and led troops in key victories in the War of 1812. While he was Governor of the new Indiana Territory, their grand mansion and farm at Vincennes was considered a wonder of the wilderness. Later, their expansive riverbank estate at North Bend, Ohio, was a landmark to river men and a friendly oasis to travelers. Their children and forty-nine grandchildren visited often.

Anna wanted her sixty-eight-year-old husband to enjoy his retirement, but a hokum-filled campaign with the slogan, "Tippecanoe and Tyler too" (John Tyler was his running mate), swept him into office and to his quick demise.

SOLEMN HONORS

Though he had not been in office long enough to make a mark on the presidency during his lifetime, President Harrison did so in death. His was the first state funeral of a president who had died in office and set the precedent for all others to follow. With no American model, the funeral designers looked to European royal funerals for ideas and came up with elaborate and dramatic arrangements. The body was prepared and placed inside a heavy mahogany coffin with a small glass pane in the lid through which the President's face could be seen. Black fabric was draped upon the coffin, the outside and the inside of the White House, and at other locations, arranged in complex swathes, rosettes, sunbursts, banners, and trimmings.

On April 7, 1841, crowds gathered outside, and a select group assembled in the East Room where the coffin was displayed amid swags and floral arrangements to hear the officiating minister intone his prayers. The coffin was taken out and placed on an imaginative funeral car, built around a curtained wagon, with four columns rising to support a roof elaborately upholstered in black and white. The coffin was set high on a draped stand beneath the intricate roof for all to see as it was pulled in the funeral procession. The Marine Band played dirges and marched behind the coffin, as military companies fired salutes. Numerous other dignitaries and marchers followed, and the coffin was taken to the Congressional Cemetery, where it was placed in a temporary vault, protected by two outer coffins and placed under guard.

During warmer weather, in late June, Harrison's coffin was carried in great ceremony to a black-swathed funeral train and conveyed to Ohio, where it was interred.

Accepting grief with dignity, Anna Harrison spent her later years living with her sole surviving child, John, father of Benjamin, who would be elected president nearly five decades after his grandfather.

Left: Harrison gained his fame at the expense of Tecumseh, the great Shawnee Indian leader who strove to unite all American Indians into a single alliance to defend their lands. Tecumseh's forces lost to Harrison at Tippecanoe in 1811 and later joined the British side in the War of 1812. This Nathaniel Currier lithograph portrays the death of Tecumseh at the 1813 Battle of the Thames River in Ontario, won by troops commanded by General Harrison. Tecumseh's death broke the league of Indian tribes.

Above: Daintily-educated Anna Harrison eloped with handsome young Harrison, choosing a frontier life of hardship, adventure, and eventual prosperity. She never had a chance to display her renowned wilderness hospitality at the White House; her husband died before she could join him in Washington.

JOHN TYLER

John Tyler

In Office
Apr. 6, 1841-Mar. 3, 1845
Born Mar. 29, 1790,
Charles City County, Va.
Party: **Whig, later Tyler**

Other Offices:
**Member, Virginia House
of Delegates, 1811-16,
1823-25, 1839
U.S. Congressman, 1817-21
Governor of Virginia, 1825-27
Chancellor, College of
William & Mary, 1859
Delegate, Confederate
Congress, 1861**

Marriages:
**Letitia Christian Tyler, 1813,
married 20 yrs.
Julia Gardiner Tyler, 1844,
married 17 yrs.**

Presidential Acts:
**Established precedent that Vice
President becomes President
upon demise or disability of
President.
Signed Webster-Ashburton
Treaty settling boundary
disputes with Canada.
Made the U.S. a participant
in policing African coast to
prevent illegal slave trading.
Signed commercial treaty
with China.
Pushed through resolution
to annex Texas.**

**Died age 71,
Jan. 18, 1862,
Richmond, Va.**

**TENTH PRESIDENT
1841-1845**
LETITIA CHRISTIAN TYLER
JULIA GARDINER TYLER

Quietly passing the time with his wife and several children at his elegant home in Williamsburg, Virginia, Vice President John Tyler had not even been informed that President Harrison was ill. When a hard-riding messenger brought him the news of the president's untimely death, Tyler was shocked. He hurriedly packed and set out on the long trip to Washington. There he faced one political crisis after another, along with personal sorrow and joy.

A SOUTHERN GENTLEMAN

Since Tyler had not been elected to the office, some thought he should be a mere acting president, but Tyler demanded—and got—recognition as president in his own right.

Right: *John Tyler was the first successor to a president who had died in office. With no precedent to guide him, he shaped the rules for all who followed in his footsteps. Tall and elegantly thin, a polished politician, he also proved to be unexpectedly romantic and prolific. He set the record for presidential offspring: fifteen.*

However, during his term, he was so often dead-locked with the Congress that not much legislation of note was passed. He vetoed so many bills that cries for his impeachment were raised—but not carried out.

Tyler was a well-educated and conservative lawyer brought up on Greenway Plantation in Virginia, son of a district judge. He worked his way up in politics to the state governorship and the U.S. Senate. A man of elite tastes, he was good-humored and loved to play the fiddle. He was devoted to his wife of twenty-seven years, Letitia, herself reared in the genteel tradition of plantation life near Greenway, daughter of a colonel.

Letitia's seven living children called her "beautiful, gentle, selfless," the guiding light of their family, even after she became partially paralyzed by a stroke. She was a frail invalid in the White House, and came downstairs only once, to see her daughter Elizabeth's wedding. She died just seventeen months after her husband became president.

Left: Vivacious Julia Tyler was a surprise choice as second wife for recently-widowed John Tyler. Young and spunky, she replaced the sombre mood in the White House following the death of Tyler's invalid first wife with dazzling glamour and fun.

THE YOUTHFUL HOSTESS

A few months later, President Tyler gave his heart to Julia Gardiner, a vivacious socialite known as "The Rose of Long Island," younger than some of his children. Astounding the nation, twenty-four-year old Julia accepted the fifty-four-year-old president's proposal. Beautiful Julia triumphantly "reigned" (as she called it) over a season of gala White House parties and balls, where she scandalized many by dancing publicly. A reporter noted, "The lovely lady Presidentress is attended on reception-days by twelve maids of honor...dressed all alike....Her serene loveliness receives upon a raised platform wearing a headress formed of bugles and resembling a crown..."

One of the most stunning evenings in White House history was Julia Tyler's Grand Finale Ball of February 18, 1845. The mansion shimmered with the light of a thousand candles as three thousand guests crowded in to greet the President and the Lady Presidentress, regally gowned in white satin ornamented with silver and diamonds. Her ostrich-plume headdress bobbed as she danced with five European ambassadors and bedazzled the love-struck chief executive.

Julia obviously adored her husband and delighted in providing him with seven children, raising his grand total to fifteen, the last born when Tyler was seventy.

Tyler died during the Civil War, and spirited Julia lived on at their Virginia plantation for nearly three more decades.

Left: While white satin adorned Washington party-goers, leather and rough homespun clothed American settlers spreading out across the continent. The struggle over Texas was a major issue of Tyler's administration, and securing the annexation of Texas was Tyler's key success. With only three days left in his term, Tyler signed a Congressional resolution calling for the admission of Texas as a

Letitia Christian Tyler

Born Nov. 12, 1790, New Kent County, Va.
Children: **5 daughters, 3 sons**

Accomplishments:
Managed complex plantation business and large family despite illness.
Died age 51, Sept. 10, 1842, White House

Julia Gardiner Tyler

Born May 4, 1820, Gardiner's Island, N.Y.
Children: **5 sons, 2 daughters**

Accomplishments:
Became first incumbent president's wife to pose for daguerreotype and to hire a press agent.
Introduced public dancing to polite society.
Championed husband's political views.
Conducted volunteer work for the Confederacy.
Raised large family.

Died age 69, Jul.10, 1889, Richmond, Va.

Above: *Industrious Sarah Polk brought fancy White House partying to a halt, instituting a sober sense of duty in all undertakings. Dubbed "Sahara Sarah," she dressed in dark tones and banned dancing and drinking hard liquor at the executive mansion.*

JAMES KNOX POLK

ELEVENTH PRESIDENT 1845-1849

SARAH CHILDRESS POLK

James Polk was president for only a single term, but during his administration the United States extended its borders from coast to coast and took on much the shape it has today. Historians consider him the only "strong" president between Jackson and Lincoln.

EXPANDING THE COUNTRY

Polk believed in Manifest Destiny—the notion that the United States had been chosen by God to guard freedom and establish hegemony over

as much of the continent as possible. In this he was supported by a public enthralled with the desire to own more territory.

Under Tyler's successor, James Polk, life at the White House lost its luster and took on a decidedly more somber, even funereal, air. Serious "godliness" was a prime concern of Mrs. Polk, a strict Presbyterian.

A dark-horse candidate, he took his electoral victory as a mandate to accomplish four goals. First, he reduced tariffs on imported goods, angering wealthy business interests but pleasing ordinary people. He established an independent treasury to safeguard public funds. He peacefully settled a potentially explosive dispute with Britain about the northern boundary of the Oregon territory, and then he moved to acquire California and the Southwest—lands controlled by Mexico.

Polk essentially triggered the Mexican War, sending American troops to the disputed areas and even into Mexico City itself. In 1848, Mexico was compelled to accept a bargain price of $15 million to give up its claim to the territories. Just a few months later, gold was discovered in California, and settlement of the west boomed.

A NEW TRADITION

Son of a prosperous farmer, Polk was a seven-term U.S. Congressman from Tennessee. His marriage to Sarah Childress, a wealthy planter's daughter, was a genuine partnership. With no children, astute, well-educated Sarah worked as her husband's private secretary and personal advisor throughout his career. She was one of the most industrious First Ladies in history. Although she allowed gaslights to be installed in the executive mansion, she greatly preferred the classic glow of candle chandeliers.

President Polk was a somber, gray-haired man, short of stature and not an impressive figure. His wife was dark-eyed and tall, perhaps a beauty by today's standards, but by those of her own day, she was not plump or rosy enough to be considered anything but "refined looking," as she was described.

Sarah was particularly concerned that her unimposing husband not escape notice in a crowded room, so she introduced the playing of "Hail to the Chief"—an old Scottish martial anthem—

to announce the President's entry. Thereafter, at crowded events, the band rolled the drums as they played the march, the people fell silent and cleared the way for the Chief Executive. This precedent has contined to the present day.

Sarah also devised an orderly manner in which numerous guests could proceed from the reception room—typically the Red Room—to the dining table. Since Jefferson's day, this had involved an awkward scramble, but Sarah plotted out a formal path proceeding into the hall, turning at the foot of the grand stairway, and continuing to the table in a dignified fashion.

Much overworked, Polk declined to run for a second term and died within a year of retirement. Sarah lived another forty-two years at their Nashville home, receiving large numbers of distinguished and ordinary callers with friendly dignity. Dressed in black and a widow's cap, she once said, "I have not sought anything. I have not travelled. I have remained at home and received what came to me. And I am satisfied with it, and am not anxious for anything more."

Above: *California gold miners search for the glitter of fortune in 1849, depicted by Currier & Ives. The gold rush began during Polk's term, giving impetus to the westward movement that would define the shape of the country.*

Right: *James Polk once called himself "the hardest-working man in the country." Although rigid and humorless, he was effective in government, expanding the nation by more than a million square miles during his single term.*

Sarah Childress Polk

Born Sept. 4, 1803, Murfreesboro, Tenn.

Children: **None**

Accomplishments:
Acted as husband's private secretary and advisor.

Died age 87, Aug. 14, 1891, Nashville, Tenn.

Right: A respected military man for more than four decades before he became president, Zachary Taylor had never held political office. His strength of conviction and character guided him during his term, cut short by death. The nation mourned his loss in a funeral procession more than two miles long witnessed by a crowd of many thousands.

Margaret (Peggy) Smith Taylor

Born Sept. 21, 1788,
Calvert Co., Md.
Children: 5 daughters, 1 son

Accomplishments:
Raised family under trying conditions of frontier military life

Died age 63, Aug. 18, 1852,
Pascagoula, Miss.

Zachary Taylor

In Office Mar. 4, 1849-Jul. 9, 1850
Born Nov. 24, 1784,
Montebello, Orange Co., Va.
Party: Whig

Early Accomplishments:
Commissioned as Army officer,
1808
Served in the War of 1812, the
Black Hawk War of 1832, the
Seminole War of 1837.
Commander, U.S. Army on the
Rio Grande in Mexican War,
1846-47.

Marriage:
Margaret M. Smith Taylor, 1810,
married 40 years.

Presidential Acts:
Oversaw Clayton-Bulwer
Treaty agreement with Britain
on potential canal rights in
Central America.
Held the line on increase in
number of slave states.

Died age 65, Jul. 9, 1850,
Washington, D.C.

ZACHARY TAYLOR

TWELFTH PRESIDENT
1849-1850
MARGARET M. SMITH TAYLOR

Both Zachary Taylor and his wife Peggy Smith Taylor were children of aristocratic Eastern families, but they spent their lives together in rough and trying circumstances on the American frontier. While Taylor pursued a forty-year military career, Peggy cheerfully raised children, fed chickens, and moved from one hardship post to another as she kept the family together. They experienced the loss of two small daughters to malaria in the bayous of Louisiana and shivered in Wisconsin outpost housing. Hardest for Peggy to bear was having to send her children back

East for their educations, not seeing them for long periods of time.

Taylor was a tough warrior but a tender and sentimental husband. He once wrote of his wife that "feminine virtues never did concentrate in a higher degree in the bosom of any woman than in hers."

"OLD ROUGH-AND-READY"

While Peggy was bearing children, Taylor distinguished himself in the War of 1812 and several other conflicts. Disdaining military uniform, he commanded his troops while wearing shabby civilian clothes topped by a farmer's wide-brimmed straw hat. He was known as "Old Rough-and-Ready" when he led his men against Mexican forces.

Fighting over rights to annex Texas, Americans and Mexicans clashed in numerous major battles. At Buena Vista, Mexico, Taylor's outnumbered troops valiantly fought the Mexicans to a standstill. Within days, Taylor became a national hero—and a pawn in the high-powered political game afoot as Polk's term ended.

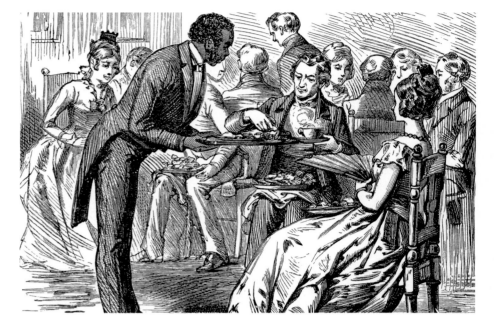

A BRIEF PRESIDENCY

Much against Peggy's wishes to trade demanding challenges for quiet retirement, Taylor accepted the Whig nomination and was elected to the presidency. Peggy responded by living an extremely private life upstairs at the White House while her youngest daughter, Betty Taylor Bliss, acted as enthusiastic hostess in her stead. Betty's manner was said to blend "the artlessness of a rustic belle and the grace of a duchess."

As president, Taylor faced the difficult question of slavery which was preoccupying the nation. He tried to facilitate the admission of California and New Mexico as free states, but just as debate was heating up, he suddenly died of gastroenteritis. The old warrior had been president just sixteen months. Cheated of quiet final years with her husband, Peggy collapsed in grief and lived but two more years.

Above: Guests at tea parties and other formal White House social events during Zachary Taylor's term were not privileged to meet the First Lady. The president's wife Peggy remained in the private quarters upstairs, where she welcomed only friends and relatives. Her youngest daughter, Betty Taylor Bliss, skillfully acted as hostess. Taylor much admired his wife, who is said never to have sat for a portrait or photograph.

Left: The war with Mexico gave General Taylor's military career a huge boost. At the 1846 Battle of Resaca de la Palma in Texas, shown here in a Nathaniel Currier lithograph, a 2,300-man army commanded by the courageous Taylor crushed 5,000 Mexican soldiers. Taylor's victories allowed him to cross the Rio Grande and invade Mexico—and made him a hero in the eyes of the American public.

Millard Fillmore

In Office
Jul. 10, 1850-Mar. 3, 1853
Born Jan. 7, 1800, Summerhill,
Cayuga County, N.Y.
Party: Whig; later American
("Know-Nothing") party

Early Offices:
N.Y. State Assemblyman,
1829-31
U. S. Congressman, 1833-35,
1837-43
Controller, New York State,
1848-49
Vice President,
March 4, 1849-July 9, 1850

Marriages:
Abigail Powers Fillmore, 1826,
married 27 yrs.
Caroline C. McIntosh Fillmore
1858, married 16 yrs.

Presidential Acts:
Enacted Henry Clay's
Compromise of 1850, attempting to reconcile pro- and anti-
slavery movements, allowing
return of escaped slaves to their
owners and abolition of slave
trade in the District of
Columbia.
Sent Commodore Perry to open
trade with Japan, defended
Hawaii from France.

Died age 74, Mar. 8, 1874,
Buffalo, N.Y.

Right: A self-made man, Millard Fillmore was the second vice president to inherit the presidency. Hard farm work took precedence over schooling in his youth, but he knew enough to guide The Compromise of 1850 into law, delaying the Civil War for more than a decade. In this portrait he wears his constant garb—a black frock coat, high-collared shirt, and a black silk neckcloth tied into a bow.

MILLARD FILLMORE

THIRTEENTH PRESIDENT
1850-1853
ABIGAIL POWERS FILLMORE

Millard Fillmore was a hard-working country youth who aspired to move beyond his humble beginnings in a log cabin in central New York State. He did so with the intelligent help of his wife Abigail, a minister's daughter who valued books and education. Much to their surprise, this somewhat ordinary couple had their hands on history for a short term in the White House.

Born on a farm, apprenticed for a time to a cloth-finisher, and barely educated, Fillmore met his future bride when he was eighteen. A handsome fellow, he walked into the classroom where lively nineteen-year-old Abigail Powers was teaching and became one of her pupils. Before too long he moved to Buffalo to find a place as a lawyer, and he and Abigail faithfully wrote to each other for several years before their marriage.

COMPROMISE AND FAILURE

Fillmore went into politics, became a U.S. Representative, and was elected Zachary Taylor's Vice President. Taylor's sudden death catapulted Fillmore to the presidency overnight. He attempted to reach compromise between pro- and anti-slavery forces in the nation and signed The Compromise of 1850, legislation that helped stave off the Civil War for several years. Abigail, who strongly opposed slavery, correctly predicted that when her husband approved a bill allowing fugitive slaves to be returned to their owners, it would spell political death for Fillmore. Indeed, Fillmore was rejected as his party's nominee when his term expired, and when he was nominated and ran for the presidency again four years later, he was soundly defeated.

WHITE HOUSE CHANGES

At the Executive Mansion, Abigail was shocked to discover no books—not even a Bible, and she persuaded Congress to give her a small sum to establish the first White House library. Intellectually curious, she held salons attended by literary greats such as Charles Dickens and Washington Irving. She also had the first bathtub and kitchen stove installed in the White House—all previous cooking had been done at a large open fireplace.

Always attentive to her family and her husband's political career, Abigail stood at Fillmore's side in the raw wind at his successor's Inauguration. Chilled to the bone, she died of pneumonia three weeks later. Tragedy soon struck again when the Fillmores' lovely eighteen-year-old daughter Mary fell victim to a fatal cholera attack.

In later years, Fillmore wed a wealthy widow and became Chancellor of the University of Buffalo.

Below: Abigail Fillmore was the first president's wife to have earned her own living—as a teacher—and to have worked outside her home after marriage. An opponent of slavery, she warned her husband against the consequences of The Compromise of 1850, which included sending fugitive slaves back to their owners.

Left: In this scene from Harriet Beecher Stowe's novel, Uncle Tom's Cabin, Little Eva and Uncle Tom share a friendship. Uncle Tom is later killed by thugs for bravely refusing to betray two fellow slaves. First published serially in an abolitionist magazine in 1851 and 1852, during Fillmore's presidency, the best-seller put a human face on the tragedy of slavery and intensified feelings that helped cause the Civil War.

Abigail Powers Fillmore

Born Mar. 13, 1798, Stillwater, N.Y.

Children: 1 son, 1 daughter

Accomplishments:
Schoolteacher before and after marriage. Established first library in the White House. Made basic improvements in White House facilities.

Died age 55, Mar. 30, 1853, Washington, D.C.

FRANKLIN PIERCE

FOURTEENTH PRESIDENT
1853-1857

JANE M. APPLETON PIERCE

A clash of thunder and a bolt of lightning brought Franklin Pierce and Jane Appleton together. Jane was rushing across the campus of Bowdoin College in Maine, when she got caught in a thunderstorm and crouched in terror under a tree. Franklin, a fellow student, dashed under the tree to rescue her. He caught her up in his arms and carried her off to romance and eventual marriage. This thrilling beginning was probably the high point of their relationship.

ATTRACTION OF OPPOSITES

Outgoing and personable, Pierce was a great success as a lawyer, congressman, and senator. He often enjoyed a drink in a tavern and loved politics. Jane was just the opposite. The daughter of a somber minister, she was fiercely religious, beset by frail health, and said to be "wanting in cheerfulness."

Too sickly to attend to domestic chores, Jane depended on hired couples to run her household. Two of her little sons died young, and she doted on her last child, Benjamin. She strongly disliked political life and Washington and was pleased when her husband retired from politics—or so she thought. He settled into practicing law in New Hampshire and even signed up to fight in the Mexican War. He came home as a General.

Humorless Jane did not know that her magnetically charming husband was secretly seeking his party's nomination for president, and when she heard that he had been nominated, she fainted with horrified shock.

SHADOW IN THE WHITE HOUSE

Shortly after Pierce's election, the final blow to Jane's composure was delivered. The president-elect, she, and their eleven-year-old son Bennie were traveling home from a family funeral by train. The couplings of the railway car snapped, and the carriage careened down an embankment. Both adults were unscathed, but their beloved son was crushed to death.

Pierce's term in office was a melancholy period for him—and for the country, as the slavery issue smoldered and threatened the union. Always shrouded in black, Jane was known as "the shadow in the White House." Official entertainment was minimal. Pierce hated abolitionists and insisted that the Constitution guaranteed owners the right to own slaves. Among Northerners, his popularity vanished.

After their Washington years, the Pierces traveled in Europe and the West Indies. Jane finally passed away, and her husband lost his personal battle with alcoholism. Though a Northerner, he publicly denounced Lincoln's policies during the Civil War.

Left: Jane Pierce was always sombre, but the tragic death of her only surviving son, Bennie, overcame her. She spent much of her time in the White House upstairs in her bedroom writing desperately sad notes to her dead son. The Executive Mansion was cold and cheerless during the Pierce administration.

Jane M. Appleton Pierce

Born Mar. 12, 1806, Hampton, N.H.
***Children:* 3 sons**

Died age 57, Dec. 2, 1863, Andover, Mass.

Franklin Pierce

In Office Mar. 4, 1853-Mar. 3, 1857
Born Nov. 23, 1804, Hillsboro, N.H.
***Party:* Democratic**

Early Offices:
N.H. State Representative & Speaker, 1829-33
U. S. Congressman, 1833-37
U. S. Senator, 1837-42

Marriage:
Jane Means Appleton Pierce, 1834, married 29 yrs.

Presidential Acts:
Signed the Kansas-Nebraska Act, allowing residents of the territories to decide whether their regions would be "slave" or "free"—thus satisfying neither side of this violently divisive issue. Concluded several treaties, including first trade treaty with Japan. Made the Gadsden Purchase of land from Mexico.

Died age 64, Oct. 8, 1869, Concord, N.H.

Left: Franklin Pierce was inaugurated at the age of forty-eight—the youngest man to become president until that time. Charming and nick-named "Handsome Frank," as president-elect he had many plans for the nation. The sudden loss of his son devastated him, and meeting the challenges of a country about to splinter apart proved too much for him.

Left: In 1856, at the Japanese port of Shimoda, America's first Consul General to Japan, Townsend Harris, is carried into town in a palanquin. Three years earlier, Commodore Matthew Perry opened Japanese ports to trade with the United States and the rest of the world. Sent out by President Fillmore, Perry reached Japan during Pierce's term. Pierce encouraged the opening of Japan, a great diplomatic achievement.

JAMES BUCHANAN

FIFTEENTH PRESIDENT
1857-1861
HARRIET LANE

James Buchanan enjoyed a distinguished forty-year career as constitutional lawyer, diplomat, congressman, and senator before he was elected president. Yet his many successes failed to enable him to find compromise between slavery and anti-slavery factions. Under his administration, the United States staggered toward Civil War.

Right: *Tall and gentle, James Buchanan proved no match for the irresistible forces impelling the nation toward Civil War. Though successful in foreign policy, in domestic policy he was like an oarsman caught in the rapids futilely trying to propel a rowboat away from the brink of Niagara Falls.*

James Buchanan

In Office
Mar. 4, 1857-Mar. 3, 1861
Born Apr. 23, 1791,
Cove Gap, PA.
Party: **Democratic**

Early Offices:
Pa. State Representative,
1814-15
U.S. Congressman, 1821-31
Minister to Russia, 1832-33
U.S. Senator, 1834-45
Secretary of State, 1845-49
Minister to Great Britain, 1853

Marriage: **None**

Presidential Acts:
Pressured Supreme Court to decide against Dred Scott, reaffirming owners' rights to slaves, vaccillated on dealing with slavery in Kansas, faced problems with John Brown's raid at Harper's Ferry and war with Mormons in Utah. Strengthened U.S. power in Latin America.

Died age 77, Jun. 1, 1868, Lancaster, PA.

Left: President Buchanan receives a delegation of Indians, inducing members of the hostile Pawnee and Ponca tribes to shake hands. As white settlers moved into their territories, Indians came under increasing pressure to give up their lands, and hostilities increased among themselves. An 1857 treaty forced the Pawnee from their villages into a small reservation in Nebraska. Harriet Lane was an ardent spokeswoman for Indian welfare, and she received many pleas for assistance from Indian tribes.

A BACHELOR PRESIDENT

The only life-long bachelor ever to occupy the White House, Buchanan was once engaged to wealthy Ann Coleman. Her parents considered him a mere fortune hunter, and gossips linked him with other women. Ann broke off the engagement and soon tragically died of an overdose of laudanum, an opium-based tranquilizer—whether by accident or intent is not known.

Buchanan's sister and brother-in-law died, leaving their young daughter Harriet Lane as Buchanan's ward. Buchanan treated Harriet like his own favored daughter, exposing her to the finest education and glimpses of diplomatic and political life. While Buchanan was envoy to Britain, Harriet became friendly with the royal family and even met Napoleon III and Empress Eugenie of France. She presented herself to Queen Victoria dressed in one hundred yards of white lace, diamond tiara, and snow-white ostrich plumes.

THE DEMOCRATIC QUEEN

As her uncle's White House hostess, pretty twenty-seven-year-old Harriet swept away the sadness of the Pierce years with gaiety and grandeur. She conferred with her uncle on matters of state, organized elegant parties, and entertained Edward, Prince of Wales. Together with Buchanan she formally received Japan's first ambassadors to the United States. Some called her the "Democratic Queen." Her name was bestowed upon children, flowers, perfumes, garments, ships, and songs. She flirtatiously brushed aside many suitors until long after her years in the Executive Mansion.

Harriet was unsympathetic to abolitionist arguments, but she advocated Native American rights. In a time of turmoil over slavery, Buchanan was no match for history. While opponents suggested that the genteel bachelor-president might be effeminate as well as ineffectual, seven states seceded and the nation began to crumble.

Harriet Lane Johnston

(President Buchanan's niece)
Born 1830, Mercersburg, PA
Marriage: 1866, to banker
Henry E. Johnston
***Children:* 2 sons**

Accomplishments:
Donated her private collection of paintings as the nucleus of the Smithsonian's National Collection of Fine Arts. Endowed still-functioning pediatric clinic at Johns Hopkins Hospital, Baltimore

Died age 73, 1903

Left: Harriet Lane Johnston was White House hostess for her bachelor uncle. Soirees, not secession, occupied the attention of the president and his niece. As war loomed, Harriet became the nation's darling, and her name ornamented everything from children to songs. Her private painting collection became the seed from which the Smithsonian's National Collection of Fine Arts grew.

ABRAHAM LINCOLN

SIXTEENTH PRESIDENT
1861-1865
MARY TODD LINCOLN

As the dark clouds of Civil War gathered over the nation, a lanky lawyer and legislator from Illinois was sworn into office. A former frontier farmer and small-time shopkeeper, Abraham Lincoln served as Commander-in-Chief during the country's most challenging crisis. Many consider him America's greatest president. His sagacious yet troubled partner in domestic and political life, Mary Todd Lincoln, made the role of First Lady conspicuous as never before. Together they shaped one of the most significant periods in American presidential history.

THE MAN FROM ILLINOIS

Sometimes the spark of genius catches fire in surprising circumstances. Lincoln was born in a dirt-floored, one-room log cabin in the backwoods of Kentucky. His illiterate father chided him for interrupting his chores with reading. His mother died when the boy was nine, and a year later his father married a widow, Sarah (Sally) Bush Johnston, who lovingly encouraged her growing stepson in his quest for learning. Lincoln added to his year of formal schooling by reading anything he could get his hands on, in between bouts of chopping wood and handyman work.

Always poor, the family moved to Indiana and on to Illinois, where Lincoln first saw the horror of slaves in chains being whipped and sold like cattle. At the rustic village of New Salem, six-foot-four-inch Lincoln clerked at the local store and read borrowed books by firelight. He and a partner went into the grocery business but incurred debts that took Lincoln fifteen years to pay off. Full of jokes and locally popular, he gained election to the Illinois assembly and was admitted to the bar.

Lincoln moved from rough-hewn society into more polished circles in the state capital. At the home of one of Springfield's more illustrious citizens, Lincoln met Mary Todd, recently graduated from a Lexington, Kentucky, finishing school, visiting her married sister. The romance between the two did not go smoothly, and they broke up for more than a year before finally marrying. They purchased a home and began their family. The marriage was one of mutual support and affection yet was always rocky. Both considered it a partnership of equals. Mary's vivaciousness and educational sophistication were assets to the couple. Had Mary not encouraged Lincoln in his quest for the presidency, he would almost certainly never have achieved the office.

Lincoln's reputation for folksy honesty and humor added to his growing stature as a politician. He became the major spokesman for limiting the expansion of slavery and in a famous speech declared that "a house divided against itself cannot stand. I believe this government cannot endure, permanently half *slave* and half *free*." He publicly debated Senator Stephen Douglas—a former beau of Mary's—on this issue in a series of crowd-pleasing encounters. Actually, Lincoln was ambivalent on slavery and only much later, with Mary's urgings, became an abolitionist.

The newly-formed Republican Party convened in Chicago in 1860 and, to wild acclaim, nominated Lincoln for the presidency. He won the election over three opponents, but joy was overshadowed by looming threats of war. Convinced that Lincoln intended to destroy the economic and political foundations of the South, southern states seceded one after the other. Lincoln and his family departed by train from Springfield for a twelve-day celebrity journey to Washington where he faced a raging turmoil.

THE YEARS OF THE WAR

At his inauguration, Lincoln declared support for states' rights and peace. He asserted, however, that the Constitution demanded that he uphold the Union at all costs, through peace or war. The South made its decision, and, on April 12, 1861, Confederate shots on Fort Sumter

---

Abraham Lincoln

In Office
Mar. 4, 1861-Apr. 15, 1865
Born Feb. 12, 1809,
Hodgenville, Hardin Co., Ky.
Party: **Republican**

Other Offices:
Volunteer, Black Hawk War,
1832.
Illinois State Representative,
1835-36.
U.S. Congressman, 1847-49.

Marriage:
Mary Ann Todd Lincoln, 1842,
married 22 yrs.

Presidential Acts:
Led the nation during the
War, 1861-65.
Issued Emancipation
Proclamation, and initiated
Thirteenth Amendment,
freeing slaves, 1862-65.
Delivered Gettysburg Address,
1863
Advocated national healing
after the Civil War.

Died age 56,
Apr. 15, 1865,
Washington, D.C.

Left: President Abraham Lincoln gazes intently into the future in this classic portrait by Alexander Gardner. The photograph was made on November 8, 1863, during the time Lincoln was writing his Gettysburg Address. As president, Lincoln faced challenges more formidable than any that had ever before beset a leader of the United States. The destiny of this great but humble man was inextricably intertwined with that of the nation.

Right: The Civil War began in 1861, when Confederate forces vigorously bombarded Fort Sumter in the harbor at Charleston, South Carolina— a state which had seceded from the Union. The shots initiated the conflict that would cost more American lives than any other war in history.

Mary Ann Todd Lincoln

Born Dec. 13, 1818, Lexington, Ky.
Children: **4 sons; one lived to maturity.**

Accomplishments:
Acted as husband's confidante and political advisor. Advocated abolition of slavery. First White House hostess to invite Black guests.

Died age 63, Jul. 16, 1882, Springfield, Ill.

Right: Mary Todd Lincoln, resplendent in a luxurious gown, Tiffany seed-pearl jewelry, and elaborate floral headdress, posed for Mathew Brady's camera near the time of the first inaugural ball in 1861. Mary was a strong force in the life of her husband—and of her country. She set out to marry a man who would be president, yet, having achieved that goal, was tormented by deep personal sorrows.

commenced the conflict that would kill 600,000 American men over the course of the next four years. The litany of disastrous encounters still brings tears of emotion to citizens of both the North and the South: Bull Run (Manassas), Shiloh, Harpers Ferry, Antietam, Chancellorsville, Fredericksburg, Vicksburg, Gettysburg, Chattanooga, Petersburg, Atlanta, Nashville, Charleston, Richmond, and finally, Appomattox, where General Robert E. Lee surrendered to General Ulysses S. Grant on April 9, 1865.

Throughout the war, grief overwhelmed the presidential family and the nation. At first, Mary was thrilled by her new position as First Lady—a term first widely used in reference to her—and she happily flaunted a lavish new wardrobe sewn of costly fabrics. She overspent the Congressional budget allowed her for redecorating the White House. As American soldiers suffered and died on the battlefields, luxury in Washington was treated harshly by the press and the public. Mary convinced Lincoln to cut out state dinners and to hold public receptions instead. Even these minimal niceties were vilified in the press. Mary paid quiet visits to military hospitals to comfort injured soldiers. Her best friend was Lizzie Keckley, her seamstress, a former slave. Mary also was the first First Lady to welcome Blacks as White House *guests*, most prominently Frederick Douglass, who was invited to tea with the president.

Then, in 1862, the Lincolns were shattered by the death of Willie, their beloved eleven-year-old son, leaving them with Robert, their eldest, and little Tad (another child, Eddie, had died in Springfield in 1850). Mary's brother Alec, a Confederate soldier, was killed in the war. For two years Mary wore only mourning black and was so upset Lincoln hinted at commiting her to a mental hospital if she could not control herself. Mary responded by stepping up her compulsive buying of luxuries, building up a personal debt of $29,000. She also actively advised the president on policy and frequently used her influence to obtain patronage posts for those in her favor. Often good-natured and charming, she was also afflicted with terrible moods. On one occasion, she made an angry public scene when the wife of a dignitary came too near Lincoln. She jealously insulted Mrs. Grant a few times.

A NATION'S TRAGEDY

Lincoln himself aged tremendously, faced as he was with mounting casualties, unsuccessful military strategists, and insubordination and virulent abuse from every quarter. His Emancipation Proclamation of 1863 was a monumental step forward for human rights but incurred much animosity from opponents.

Above: *The greatest battle ever fought in the Western hemisphere took place at Gettysburg, Pennsylvania, July 1-3, 1863, marking the turning point of the Civil War. Union forces of 90,000 drove back 75,000 Confederate men in a fiery clash, leaving more than 5,000 dead upon the battlefield. Lincoln grieved deeply over the losses.*

Union military successes led to Lincoln's reelection and the end of the war. Lincoln spoke from a White House window to delirious victory throngs, calling for mutual understanding in the rebuilding of the nation. Four days later, on Good Friday, April 14, 1865, rejoicing at last in peace, the Lincolns went to see a comedy at Ford's Theater. A disgruntled pro-slavery actor, John Wilkes Booth, burst into the unguarded presidential box to fire a bullet into Lincoln's brain. The president never regained consciousness and died the next morning at 7:22 a.m. As he breathed his last, the weeping Secretary of War, Edward M. Stanton, whispered, "Now he belongs to the ages." Mary was hysterical and stricken with grief beyond measure.

Lincoln's body lay in state in the East Room of the White House on a black-draped catafalque—a scene Lincoln himself had envisioned in a nightmare not long before. Thousands of weeping mourners filed past. Thousands more turned out to witness the slow passage of the funeral train across the country to Lincoln's final resting place in Springfield, Illinois. The man who rose from the humblest of beginnings to inspire a nation and the world had met his destiny.

Mary lived another seventeen years, facing constant financial problems, mental imbalance, and more grief—her son Tad died of tuberculosis at eighteen. She lived in Europe for some years and became involved with spiritualism. Robert, her sole surviving son, had her declared insane. After much-needed psychiatric care, Mary had the judgment reversed and reconciled with Robert. She spent her final days in Springfield, endlessly repacking her sixty-four trunks of elegant fabrics, and died in the house where she had married the man beside whom she stood during some of the most crucial moments in American history.

THE WARM-HEARTED MR. LINCOLN

A distraught mother came to the White House to plead for her young son, condemned for sleeping at his military post. Lincoln scrawled out a pardon and handed it to the woman. As she left, the woman exclaimed to her escort, "I knew it was a lie! When I left home yesterday, my neighbors told me that I would find Mr. Lincoln an ugly man. It was a lie; he is the handsomest man I ever saw in my life!"

Right: Lincoln and his youngest son, Tad, examine a family album together. Anthony Berger, a photographer at Mathew Brady's Washington studio recorded the moment on February 9, 1864, the only time Lincoln ever posed with a member of his family. Of the Lincolns' four children, only Robert, the eldest, survived to adulthood.

MR. LINCOLN, THE STATESMAN:

"Four score and seven years ago our fathers brought forth on this continent, a new nation, conceived in Liberty, and dedicated to the proposition that all men are created equal....

-that this nation, under God, shall have a new birth of freedom—and that government of the people, by the people, for the people, shall not perish from the earth."

From the Gettysberg Address, November 19, 1863.

"With malice toward none, with charity for all; with firmness in the right, as God gives us to see the right, let us strive on to finish the work we are in; to bind up the nation's wounds; . . . to do all which may achieve and cherish a just, and a lasting, peace, among ourselves, and with all nations."

From Lincoln's Second Inaugural Address, March 4, 1865.

Left: Lincoln's assassin dashes across the stage at Ford's Theater, April 14, 1865, his victim fatally wounded in the box above.
John Wilkes Booth, one of the best-known actors of the day, shot Lincoln in the head from the rear of the presidential box, then leapt down to his escape. Booth was later killed and several conspirators executed.

Right: Fate handed Andrew Johnson the leadership of the United States in very troubled times. A southerner loyal to the Union, Johnson was a man of simple background and conscience. He tried to bring harmony to a nation recovering from Civil War, but he and his plans fell victim to unscrupulous politicians out for blood.

Andrew Johnson

In Office
Apr.15, 1865-Mar. 3, 1869
Born Dec. 29, 1808, Raleigh, N.C.
Party: **Democratic**

Other Offices:
Greeneville town alderman & mayor, 1828-33.
Member, Tennessee Legislature, 1835-37, 1839-41.
Tennessee State Senator, 1841.
U.S. Congressman, 1843-53.
Governor of Tennessee, 1853-57.
U.S. Senator, 1857-62, 1875.
Military Governor of Tennessee, 1862-65.

Marriage:
Eliza McCardle Johnson, 1827, married 48 yrs.

Presidential Acts:
Oversaw Fourteenth Amendment to the Constitution, granting citizenship to all born and naturalized, 1868.
Oversaw Fifteenth Amendment to the Constitution, providing voting rights to all races, 1869.
Opposed Congressional efforts to disenfranchise southern whites, vetoed unconstitutional legislation.
Oversaw purchase by Sec. of State Seward of Alaska from Russia for $7,200,000, 1867.
Championed the common worker.

Died age 66, Jul. 31, 1875, Carter's Station, Tenn.

ANDREW JOHNSON

SEVENTEENTH PRESIDENT
1865-1869
ELIZA MCCARDLE JOHNSON

When Lincoln sought reelection in 1864, he chose as his running mate Andrew Johnson of Tennessee, the only southern senator loyal to the Union. The balanced ticket was a winner, but for Johnson, fate in the form of John Wilkes Booth brought him more than he had bargained for. Within days of the inauguration, the stunned and grieving Johnson was hastily sworn in as president.

A CONSTITUTIONAL VICTORY

Johnson's tragedy was that he was a Jackson Democrat in a Republican administration, and the so-called Radical Republicans aimed to destroy Democratic power in the South. They wanted to get rid of Johnson so they could deprive southern whites of the vote and push newly-freed Blacks into office. Where they succeeded, they sowed the seeds of hatred, and the Ku Klux Klan began to ride. Johnson battled to continue Lincoln's magnanimous policy of conciliation and vetoed these propositions. Locked in combat with a Congress that sought to trample on the Constitution, Johnson became the only president ever to be impeached—that is, indicted—escaping conviction on trumped up charges designed to oust him from office, by only one vote. Modest Johnson's victory proved to be an historic victory for the nation and the Constitution.

HUMBLE BEGINNINGS

Johnson began life in a shack in North Carolina, and his father died when he was a toddler. He worked as a tailor's apprentice and then a tailor, with no time for schooling. When a friendly customer read to him, however, young Andy became intrigued and gradually taught himself to read. He and his family moved in a rattle-trap cart across the Great Smokies to Greeneville, a poor eastern Tennessee mountain village, where he met Eliza McCardle, daughter of a cobbler and his widow who made cloth-topped sandals for a living. The teenagers soon married and began a harmonious life together, producing five children. Genial Eliza happily shared her good basic education with her serious husband and encouraged him to learn more. Always proud of his background as a poor workingman, he was politically ambitious and rose from town mayor to state governor and U.S. Senator.

Like many in eastern Tennessee, he opposed secession, although his state joined the Confederacy. When the Confederate government withdrew from Nashville in 1862, Lincoln sent Johnson there as military governor, where he oversaw Reconstruction. He learned firsthand the value of moderation and reason in rebuilding the Union—a view he brought to the White House.

When Eliza suddenly became First Lady, she moved to the Executive Mansion with twelve family members, including children and grandchildren. She herself was in such poor health that she delegated all hostessing duties to her charming daughter Martha Patterson, married to a senator. The entire family was unpretentious and gentle, and Martha successfully oversaw many parties, despite the tension of the ill-fated impeachment proceedings.

VINDICATED AT LAST

After Johnson's term, Eliza returned with relief to the family home in Tennessee. She lived to see her husband reelected to the U.S. Senate—the only former president to serve as Senator—where he found his desk covered with flowers and the hands of repentant legislators stretched out in welcome. Both Johnson and Eliza died within a year of their happy vindication.

Right: Newly-freed Blacks cast their votes at a southern polling station during the 1867 state elections, as depicted in Harper's Weekly. Radical Republican northern politicians wanted southern Blacks to vote, but cynically sought to deprive southern Whites of the vote so the northern Whites would not be outnumbered in Congress. Johnson wanted the vote for all sectors—and clashes over this issue led to his impeachment.

Below: *No haughty airs came with Eliza Johnson to the White House. A cobbler's daughter, she took more pleasure in having her large family around her in the Executive Mansion than in fancy entertainments. Her daughter, Martha Johnson Patterson, who often acted as White House hostess, declared modestly, "We are plain people, from the mountains of Tennessee, called here for a short time by a national calamity. I trust too much will not be expected of us."*

Eliza McCardle Johnson

Born Oct. 4, 1810, Leesburg, Tenn.
Children: 3 sons, 2 daughters

Accomplishments:
Taught her husband writing and speaking skills essential to his career.
Oversaw harmonious family life.

Died age 65, Jan. 15, 1876, Greene County, Tenn.

Ulysses Simpson Grant

In Office
Mar. 4, 1869-Mar. 3, 1877
Born Apr. 27, 1822,
Point Pleasant, Ohio
Party: Republican

Other Offices:
U.S. Army officer, 1843-53,
1861-66.
General of the Army, 1866.
Secretary of War, 1867-68 (apptd.)

Marriage:
Julia Boggs Dent Grant, 1848,
married 36 yrs.

Presidential Acts:
Faced "Black Friday" Gold Crisis.
Oversaw anti-Ku Klux Klan Act,
1871.
General Amnesty act for former
Confederates, 1872.
Appointed talented Hamilton Fish
Secretary of State, 1869, who set-
tled boundaries with Canada.

Died age 63, Jul. 23, 1885,
Mount McGregor, N.Y.

ULYSSES S. GRANT

EIGHTEENTH PRESIDENT
1869-1877
JULIA DENT GRANT

Few men have been as popular as General Ulysses S. Grant when sworn in as president. The American people acclaimed him for winning the war for the North and treating the South with magnanimity. His inauguration was a moment of great triumph for a man who had won over many obstacles—not the least of which was himself. As Grant and his ever-faithful wife Julia joyously entered the White House, they must have reflected that eight years earlier, Grant had been a down-on-his-luck clerk in a leather store, unloading boxes and taking orders from his younger brothers. His rise had been meteoric indeed.

FROM FAILURE TO SUCCESS

Urged by his father to attend West Point, Grant was a lackluster student and mediocre army officer. He saw action in the Mexican War, where he privately decried American imperialism against the impoverished Mexicans. One of the few who saw much promise in Grant was Julia Dent, sister of his West Point roommate, the plain cross-eyed daughter of a prosperous St. Louis family. Julia owned three slaves herself, which outraged Grant's anti-slavery father, who refused to attend the wedding.

The young couple, with their increasing family—three sons and a little girl—traveled from one military post to another, bound together by long-lasting affection. Unfortunately, Grant could not tolerate alcohol, and his public drunkenness led to his forced resignation from the army. In private life, he suffered a series of business failures, finally begging his father for the store clerk job in Galena, Illinois.

The Civil War changed Grant's luck. He managed to secure a regimental command and gave the Union armies their first important victory at Fort Henry. At Fort Donelson he earned his army nickname, "Unconditional Surrender," which was what he demanded of the Confederates there. He assumed complete command of the U.S. armies, won more key victories, and accepted Lee's surrender, concurring with Lincoln in allowing the Confederates to honorably lay down their arms without retribution.

As president, Grant proved yet again that he had few skills beyond the battlefield. His naive failure to control the schemers around him led to outrageous scandals that

Left: *Lieutenant General Ulysses S. Grant pauses for a moment outside his tent during the siege of Petersburg, Virginia, which lasted nearly ten months in 1864-1865. Grant seemed destined for a life of hard luck, but his dramatic Civil War military victories swept him into the presidency on a wave of popular acclaim. His administration was rocked by corruption he could not control.*

Right: *A tumultuous greeting from huge crowds and a grand reception at the Palace Hotel in San Francisco saluted the Grants when they returned from a two-and-a-half-year world tour in 1879. The Grants were feted like royalty in Europe, the Middle East, India, China, and Japan, yet met an even warmer welcome upon reaching home. An effort to nominate the old soldier for yet another presidential term fizzled.*

rocked his administration. Swindling financiers and entrepreneurs colluded at every level around the good-natured Grant, as the nation entered a period of untrammeled industrial growth and speculation. The Sioux nation, angered by prospectors flooding into their territory, masssacred Custer's troops at Little Big Horn, but they, like Grant, were powerless to stop the corrupt expansionism afflicting the nation. The South reeled from carpetbaggers and vengeful policies. For some, this brash era was the "Gilded Age."

LIVING IN HIGH STYLE

At the White House, Grant and Julia enjoyed the happiest time of their lives. Julia read the president's mail and advised him on appointments. She believed her position obliged her to be a public personality, and she was the first First Lady to issue press releases. Swathed in bustled silk dresses, she delighted in organizing grandiose twenty-nine-course dinners, pepped up with her champagne and Cointreau punch (served despite her husband's continuing alcohol problem). She gave daytime receptions for ladies of all social levels, where she was proud of the fact that maids and countesses rubbed elbows.

She reveled in her pretty daughter Nellie's wedding to an Englishman—later shown to be a cad—one of the grandest occasions ever celebrated at the mansion. The East Room was smothered in white roses, and Nellie wore white satin and a $2,000 rose-point veil ordered from Brussels. Julia wept when the day came to leave Washington. Later, she said, "My life at the White House was like a bright and beautiful dream...a garden spot of orchids, and I wish it might have continued forever...."

The Grants continued their grandiose lifestyle on a lengthy grand tour; reigning monarchs and nobles entertained them lavishly in every nation from England to Japan. Coming home was hard; in New York, the Grants were swindled out of all their funds and left penniless. Struggling with throat cancer, Grant penned his memoirs, securing at last, after his death, financial security for Julia, who lived handsomely on the $450,000 proceeds for seventeen years.

Above: Always loyal to her husband through failure and success, Julia Dent Grant delighted in her days at the White House, which were "like a bright and beautiful dream." Casting aside memories of days of penury, she donned jewels, silks, and lace at her lavish entertainments. Because of an eye defect, she never gazed directly into the camera. Grant declared that he loved her with her eyes just the way they were.

Julia Dent Grant

**Born Jan. 26, 1826,
St. Louis, Mo.**
Children: **3 sons, 1 daughter**

Accomplishments:
Husband's personal and political partner, tended to home life.

**Died age 76,
Dec. 14, 1902,
Washington, D.C.**

RUTHERFORD B. HAYES

NINETEENTH PRESIDENT
1877-1881
LUCY W. WEBB HAYES

A gentleman of honesty and principle, Rutherford B. Hayes was always a proponent of doing what was right. He enjoyed the love of a woman of fine character and of his well-behaved offspring and was elected to the highest office in the land. He lacked but one thing: charisma. Hayes diligently carried out his duties at a quiet time in history, when Americans wanted to ignore government and get on with business growth, inventiveness, and expansion to the West.

AN UPSTANDING COUPLE

Hayes was a lawyer and Civil War hero elected to Congress without campaigning—he declared that any officer who would take leave from the field of battle to campaign should be scalped. Later governor of his native Ohio, he became a Republican compromise presidential candidate whose election was sullied by wheeling and dealing over electoral votes for months after the popular election. Not until the last minute did Hayes know that he would be inaugurated—which he was, twice—first privately, and again before thousands of onlookers.

Inspiring self-confidence in Hayes was his plainly-garbed wife Lucy—who eschewed personal vanity, including all fashion and beauty aids. Her severe hair-do hinted at her character—upright, defender of traditional family bonds, devoted mother, and proponent of temperance. Personally warm and kind, Lucy began the tradition of Easter-egg rolling on the White House lawn. Lucy and her husband ordered that no alcohol be served in the mansion, but a steward is rumored to have once slipped some rum into a special sherbet for a favored few.

Both Hayes and Lucy had lost their fathers virtually at birth and were reared by

Right: Honest strength of character was Rutherford B. Hayes's strong point, although inspiring leadership was not. A proud Civil War veteran who had been wounded several times, he followed a policy of reconciliation toward the South. At the end of his term, he was relieved to return to obscure private life.

their mothers and helpful relatives. Hayes's uncle sent him to Harvard Law School and left him a fortune. Lucy's mother enabled her to graduate from Wesleyan Female College in 1851—she was the first college graduate to serve as First Lady. When her husband was wounded in the Civil War, she visited the hospital to care for him and other wounded men, earning their deep devotion. The couple lovingly raised five children (three more youngsters died) and began and ended each day with family prayers and Methodist hymns. Lucy charmed women journalists, one of whom likened her to the Madonna, although another journalist accused her of being too exalted to speak out in favor of women's education.

FIRST FAMILY ENTERTAINMENTS

Lucy hated formal dinners, but she arranged a splendid Blue Room wedding in 1878 for Hayes's niece, Emily Platt. Her most sentimental party marked her own silver wedding anniversary, in which Hayes and Lucy reenacted their marriage, complete with the original minister and wedding dress. A grand reception followed, with the presidential couple greeting friends under a wedding bell of white blossoms. On another occasion, an invitation to Helen Herron, daughter of Hayes's former law partner, changed the course of the young woman's life: she vowed to return one day as First Lady herself. She did—as Mrs. Taft.

The telephone, typewriter, and a permanent running-water system made their appearance in the White House during the Hayes years. The couple traveled more than any predecessors had while in office, and Hayes was the first president to visit the West coast.

Returning to Ohio and their family home, Hayes and Lucy remained active for many years, engaged in a variety of causes, surrounded by their children and many visitors.

Below: Lucy Webb Hayes gained note as "Lemonade Lucy," because of her firm prohibition on serving alcohol in the White House. She and Hayes brought family prayers and nightly hymns to the Executive Mansion, and she was a heroine of the Women's Christian Temperance Union, which commissioned this portrait. Lucy was the first college graduate to serve as First Lady.

Right: Like Joan of Arc battling the enemy, American women fought to abolish the consumption of alcohol, as depicted in this Currier & Ives print of 1874. During the 1870s, thousands of women church members went into saloons, sang hymns and prayed, persuading barkeepers to close down. The Temperance Crusade swept over twenty-three states— finally resulting in national Prohibition from 1920 to 1933.

Lucy Ware Webb Hayes

Born Aug. 28, 1831, Chillicothe, Ohio
Children: **7 sons, 1 daughter (5 lived past childhood)**

Accomplishments:
First college graduate to serve as First Lady. Advocated temperance. Raised large family and supported husband.

Died age 57, Jun. 25, 1889, Fremont, Ohio

JAMES A. GARFIELD

TWENTIETH PRESIDENT
1881
LUCRETIA RUDOLPH GARFIELD

At the 1880 Republican convention, Senator-elect James A. Garfield took the podium to speak in oratorical tones in favor of the nomination of his friend John Sherman for president. Sherman failed to win the balloting—but Garfield did; he himself became the "dark horse" nominee. Garfield had been in Congress for eighteen years yet was unbesmirched by the scandals that touched nearly every other politician of the time. He easily won the election and was moving toward governmental reform when fate prematurely stayed his hand.

Above: Crete Garfield shared love and wisdom with her charismatic husband, guiding him away from political corruption. Suffering from malaria, the First Lady is here helped down the White House stairs for an evening carriage ride. On June 18, 1881, as Garfield escorted her to the train station to send her to recover at the shore, the assassin stalking him held his fire. "Mrs. Garfield looked so thin, and she clung so tenderly to the President's arm, that I did not have the heart to fire upon him," the criminal later wrote.

Below: The stalker, a disappointed job-seeker, finally struck on July 2, and Garfield died on September 19, 1881. More than 100,000 silent mourners filed past President Garfield's illuminated catafalque.

FAITH AND HARD WORK

The last of the presidents to have grown up in a log cabin, young Garfield had known hungry poverty. His homesteading father died at thirty-three, leaving his mother to raise four children, James but a toddler. James cut wood, boiled salts, drove boats on the Ohio canal—and got an education in a Bible school. He managed to graduate from Williams College in Massachusetts and returned to teach Latin, Greek, history, philosophy, mathematics, and English at his old school, the Eclectic Institute in Hiram, Ohio. There he courted and wed a fellow member of the Church of the Disciples, dainty but dynamic Lucretia "Crete" Rudolph, who like others in the community, admired Garfield's magnetic evangelical style.

While the industrious Garfield studied law, got himself elected to the Ohio Senate, valiantly led troops in the Civil War, and was elected to Congress, Crete gave birth to the first two of their seven children. The first, a little daughter, and the last, an infant son, died.

For nearly two decades, the family lived in Washington but every summer traveled to Ohio, where they puttered around their farm. Doting parents, the Garfields educated their children at home. Crete's protective wisdom helped her husband avoid the moral pitfalls politics offered in those corruption-ridden years. Their deep mutual love enabled them to overcome marital difficulties presented by Garfield's liaison with a New York woman. Crete believed that women ought to think of themselves as the equal of men.

After Garfield took office as president, crowds of strangers surged into the White House to attend receptions and ask for patronage jobs. Once a shy country girl, Crete was a poised hostess and her husband's astute political adviser, but a hot-weather attack of malaria kept her in bed for four weeks. To help her recuperate, Garfield rented a summer cottage on the New Jersey shore and moved her there with the family.

THE SECOND ASSASSINATION

Garfield unhesitatingly attacked corruption in the New York Custom House and the Post Office, and planned an address at his alma mater, Williams College. On July 2, Garfield went to the Washington station to catch his train, and there a disappointed office seeker who had been stalking him, lawyer Charles Guiteau, stepped out of the crowd

James Abram Garfield

In Office
Mar. 4, 1881-Sept. 19, 1881
Born Nov. 19, 1831,
Orange, Ohio
Party: **Republican**

Other Offices:
President, Hiram College, Ohio,
1857-61.
Ohio State Senator, 1859.
Served in the Civil War,
brigadier general, 1861-63.
U.S. Congressman, 1862-80.

Marriage:
Lucretia Rudolph Garfield,
1858, married 26 yrs.

Presidential Acts:
Fought government corruption,
especially in N.Y. Customs and
the Post Office.

Died age 49, Sept. 19, 1881,
Elberon, N.J.

Left: James A. Garfield's background as a hard-working farmer, devout preacher, Civil War hero, and honest politician convinced American voters to put him in the White House. His attacks on corruption were tragically cut short by an assassin's bullet and inept medical care.

and shot twice. One bullet grazed the president's arm, but another lodged in his back, harmlessly encysting itself.

Garfield lay weak but alert in the muggy White House for two months while doctors unnecessarily probed his wound with unsterile implements and his wife lovingly nursed him. He asked to be taken to the shore, hoping the ocean air would restore his health. Sadly, even the sea breezes could not overcome the infection introduced by the doctors, and Garfield died, six months after his inauguration. As the enormity of his murder struck her, his wife lamented, "Oh, why am I made to suffer this cruel wrong!"

Crete carried herself with dignity during the elaborate state funeral and the return of Garfield to Cleveland for burial. A public subscription amounting to $300,000 was raised, enabling her to provide for her children. The assassin was hanged.

The year after Crete was widowed, a rumor circulated that she would marry again. She was horrified and emphatically declared that she could never forget "that I am the wife of General Garfield." She lived in honorable privacy for another thirty-six years.

Lucretia Rudolph Garfield

Born Apr. 19, 1832,
Hiram, Ohio
Children: **5 sons, 2 daughters**
(2 died young)

Accomplishments:
Taught school.
Successfully raised large family,
supported husband's efforts.
Planned cultural programs
and historic restoration of the
White House.

Died age 85, Mar. 14, 1918,
Pasadena, Calif.

CHESTER A. ARTHUR

TWENTY-FIRST PRESIDENT
1881-1885

"Chet Arthur, President of the United States! Good God!" exclaimed one observer when news of President Garfield's death became known. Vice President Arthur's name had been tangled up in charges of corruption leveled at New York state politicians, especially the ruthless political boss New York Senator Roscoe Conkling, Arthur's political mentor. Arthur had been put on the ticket with Garfield merely to keep Conkling from making trouble. No one considered the possibility that this questionable lawyer could actually become president.

Chester Alan Arthur

In Office
Sept. 20, 1881-Mar. 3, 1885
Born Oct. 5, 1829, Fairfield, Vt.
Party: **Republican**

Other Offices:
Judge Advocate of Militia,
New York State, 1857.
Quartermaster General of New
York, Chief Engineer of Militia
on Governor's Staff, 1862.
Collector of the Port of New
York, 1871-78 (removed by
order of President Hayes).

Marriage:
Ellen Lewis Herndon Arthur,
1859, married 20 yrs.

Children: **2 sons, 1 daughter**
(Born 1837, Died 1880)

Presidential Acts:
Prosecuted culprits in Star
Route Post Office Frauds.
Enacted Pendleton Civil Service
Act, 1883, launching important
civil service reform.

Died age 57, Nov. 18, 1886,
New York, N.Y.

Right: *Chester A. Arthur surprised everyone by shucking off his questionable political past to become a conscientious president. He helped push through legislation to punish government officials demanding salary kickbacks from employees. Posing for his portrait in a fur-trimmed coat, Arthur enjoyed elegance in clothing and furnishings.*

But become president he did, and he helped see to it that Garfield's murderer was executed. He surprised everyone by sloughing off his past to become an ardent advocate of reform in the civil service system, and he completed his presidential term with honesty and credibility.

LIFE IN NEW YORK

Arthur was born in Vermont, one of nine children of a Baptist preacher who had immigrated from Northern Ireland. The family lived frugally as they traveled from one post to another. Arthur graduated from Union College, became a teacher, and then a lawyer—just one of many young attorneys seeking their fortunes in New York City.

A friend introduced him to graceful Ellen (Nell) Herndon, daughter of a naval Captain who heroically went down with his ship in a storm off Cape Hatteras. Nell's roots were in the Virginia aristocracy, and family ties made her a Rebel sympathizer. The tall handsome lawyer, by now a rising politician, married her in 1859, solidifying a romantic, sunny union.

As assistant quartermaster general in New York during the Civil War, Arthur efficiently supplied and housed thousands of troops. Linking himself to Boss Conkling, head of one of the most efficient political organizations ever, Arthur prospered as Collector at the corrupt New York Custom House. Amazingly, he himself maintained an upright reputation and was received in the highest society.

Nell and Arthur were a lively, popular pair, and they produced two sons—the firstborn died— and a daughter, little Nell. At their fashionably furnished Lexington Avenue brownstone, they entertained Roosevelts and Vanderbilts. Nell wore Tiffany jewelry and was an accomplished concert singer. It was while waiting for her carriage after a performance that she caught pneumonia, killing her at forty-two, the year before her husband's surprising leap to the presidency.

THE ABSENT FIRST LADY

Arthur mourned his wife deeply and each day placed fresh roses before her portrait at his bedside in the White House. In her memory, he donated a stained glass window to St. John's Church, where she had sung in the choir as a young woman, and had it placed so he could see it at shining at night from the White House. Speaking of life without Nell, he confessed, "Honors to me now are not what they once were." He never allowed anyone else to take her place, although his youngest sister, Mary McElroy, entertained elegantly at the mansion each winter season. At other times, Arthur himself organized social events. Dinners, with wine, were reputed to be excellent. For his family, Arthur emphasized privacy, and little Nell was glimpsed only occasionally, taking sedate drives with her father. For this motherless household, there was little gaiety.

Elegant Arthur was appalled at the White House furnishings and had twenty-four wagonloads of decorations and furniture—some of it priceless—auctioned off. He had the mansion completely redone in late-Victorian style.

Arthur was considered one of the country's best fishermen; he once hooked an eighty-pound bass off the Rhode Island coast. In 1883, he camped, fished and rode horseback through Wyoming to Yellowstone Park, a much-needed tonic for the exhausted president.

Arthur left office after astonishing his old cronies and the nation with his excellent performance. Within two years, however, he fell victim to fatal kidney and heart disease.

Below: Ellen Herndon Arthur, known as Nell, died before her husband became president. Arthur adored her and wrote to her, before they were married, "I know you are thinking of me. I feel the pulses of your love answering to mine. If I were with you now, you would go & sing for me 'Robin Adair,' then you would . . . put your arms around my neck and press your soft sweet lips over my eyes. I can feel them now."

Left: A group of emigrants, seeking a new destiny in America, clusters at a European quay, waiting to leave for New York. During the 1880s, a major wave of immigration to the United States began, with most new arrivals coming from Europe. President Arthur's father was an immigrant from Northern Ireland.

(Stephen) Grover Cleveland

In Office Mar. 4, 1885-Mar. 3, 1889, Mar. 4, 1893-Mar. 3, 1897
Born Mar. 18, 1837, Caldwell, N.J.
***Party:* Democratic**

Other Offices:
Assistant District Attorney, Erie Co., N.Y., 1863-65.
Erie Co. Sheriff, 1871-73.
Mayor of Buffalo, N.Y., 1882.
Governor of New York, 1883-85.
Trustee, Princeton University, 1901.

Marriage:
Frances Folsom Cleveland, 1886, married 22 yrs.

Presidential Acts:
Repealed Sherman Silver Purchase Law, 1893.
Passed anti-tariff measures, 1894.
Broke up Coxey's March of unemployed, 1894.
Quelled Pullman railroad strike, 1894.
Recovered public lands claimed by railroads.
Limited Civil War Pension grab.
Settled Venezuela-British Guiana boundary dispute, 1895-99.
Refused to annex Hawaii against Hawaiian wishes, 1891.
Oversaw Interstate Commerce Act, 1887.

Died age 71, Jun. 24, 1908, Princeton, N.J.

GROVER CLEVELAND

TWENTY-SECOND AND TWENTY-FOURTH PRESIDENT
1885-1889, 1893-1897
FRANCES FOLSOM CLEVELAND

A hefty 250-pound man sometimes likened to a walrus, Grover Cleveland tallied up some important firsts. He was the first Democrat elected to the White House since before the Civil War, the first man to leave the presidency and return to it later, and the first incumbent president to be married at the White House. He was known for a no-nonsense "ugly-honest" approach which pleased some but greatly angered others. He was so stubborn some called him "His Obstinacy." For all of his own unique qualities, however, he was most celebrated as the husband of a beautiful woman, the youngest First Lady.

HONESTY ABOVE ALL

Cleveland was fifth of nine children of a Presbyterian minister, raised in upstate New York. His father died when he was a teenager, and he supported his mother and younger sisters, paying a substitute to take his place in the Civil War (a common practice). As Erie County Sheriff, he was noted for complete honesty and lusty relaxation in beer-hall society. He single-mindedly rose to the top in politics—Mayor of Buffalo, Governor of New York, and, backed by both Democrats and reform Republicans—the "Mugwumps"—the presidency. During his campaign, a woman claimed he had fathered her illegitimate son. "Tell the truth," he told his people; he admitted he

Left: The wedding of President Cleveland and Frances Folsom was held June 2, 1886, in the Blue Room, adorned with a bower of pansies and red roses and a ship of pink rosebuds and pansies. Five wagonloads of roses, azaleas, geraniums, and heliotropes festooned other parts of the mansion. Cabinet members and a few close friends witnessed the union of the young bride, resplendent in ivory satin edged with orange blossoms and veiled in silk tulle, with her proud groom, twenty-seven years her senior.

night have sired the boy. Sloganeers chanted, "Ma! Ma! Where's my pa? Gone to the White House, Ha! Ha! Ha!" Cleveland won anyway.

As president, rooting out graft and fiscal abuse from dirty government was his specialty. He staunchly upheld the gold standard, attacked tariffs, and tried to stem the tide of the panic of 1893. Surprisingly unsympathetic to the workers' plight, he sent federal troops to break up the huge Pullman Strike, led by Eugene V. Debs, and pitted police against hundreds of unemployed demonstrators in Washington.

A bachelor in the White House, Cleveland missed his beer, sausages, and poker. For a while, he had his sister Rose Cleveland act as hostess in her own plain way. But Cleveland had bigger plans. For years, he had secretly courted his deceased law partner's young daughter, writing to her at college (with her mother's permission). He had known her since she was an infant and had seen her grow up in privileged Buffalo society. At twenty-one, Frances (Frank) Folsom was a dark-eyed beauty. She and her mother traveled to Europe to buy her trousseau, and on their arrival in New York harbor were set upon by the press. From that moment forward, the press was incredibly aggressive, printing stories true and brassily false about her, feeding what would become a national obsession with Frances.

Below: Beautiful Frances Folsom Cleveland captured the nation's heart in a time of ecomomic depression. Twenty-one when she became First Lady, Frances was still lovely at thirty-five when Anders Zorn painted her in 1899. As mistress of the Executive Mansion and devoted wife, lively Frances was a spectacular success.

MOST-POPULAR FIRST LADY

Cleveland wrote out invitations to a privileged few but four days before the June, 1886 wedding. Guests stood amid bowers of flowers to hear John Philip Sousa lead the Marine Band in Mendelssohn's "Wedding March" and see the lovely bride gracefully descend the grand staircase on the arm of her somewhat paunchy groom. At the reception, telegrams from Queen Victoria and other notables were read, and the couple set out for their honeymoon at Deer Park in Maryland.

The press bedeviled their every move there and for years afterward, using spyglasses, bribery, and their imaginations in creating their tales. Without her permission, Frances' likeness was used on commercial products of every sort. Gawking crowds shoved to glimpse her everywhere she went.

Frances won public adoration on an unprecedented scale. Her influence even softened her husband. All thought her brilliant, affable, charming, naturally cordial, and delightful. She held two weekly afternoon receptions, one considerately held on Saturday when women with jobs were free to come. She shook hands with thousands of women of all classes and ethnicities. Her formal entertainments were grand occasions, and she worked to further women's education.

During the four years Cleveland was out of office, Frances gave birth to Baby Ruth (after whom the candy bar was named). Later, Esther became the first presidential child born in the White House; then Marion appeared. Much later two boys were born, and Ruth died of diphtheria. The children had to be protected from aggressive admirers.

Frances was the very model of a happy wife, nursing her husband through a frightening bout with jaw cancer, and responding to his tenderness. In response to a false report of domestic strife, she issued a press release: "I can wish the women of our country no better blessing than that their homes and their lives may be as happy, and that their husbands may be as kind and attentive, as considerate and affectionate, as mine."

The Clevelands spent their latter years in Princeton, N.J., much in social demand. He became a respected elder statesman and was adjudged a "near-great" president. Five years after Cleveland's demise, Frances married a Princeton archaeology professor, T.J. Preston, Jr. She lived into her eighties, the most popular woman ever to serve as the nation's hostess.

Frances Folsom Cleveland

Born Jul. 21, 1864, Folsomville, N.Y.
Children: **3 daughters, 2 sons**

Accomplishments:
Youngest White House hostess. Successfully raised family in glare of publicity. Advocated improved education for women.

Died age 83, Oct. 29, 1947, Baltimore, Md.

BENJAMIN HARRISON

TWENTY-THIRD PRESIDENT
1889-1893

CAROLINE L. SCOTT HARRISON

Between the colorful Clevelands' two terms in the White House, the Executive Mansion was occupied for four years by Benjamin and Caroline Harrison—nice folks, but relatively dull. In fact, Theodore Roosevelt called Harrison "the little grey man."

HARRISON AS PRESIDENT

Usually cold to people outside his family, Harrison was raised in genteel poverty in Ohio. He met his future wife when they were students at Miami University in Ohio, known as the "Yale of the West." Caroline, or Carrie, was all that strait-laced Ben was not—sociable and warm. Both short of stature, they fell in love and worked together in the early years of their marriage to overcome poverty as they raised their two small children in Indianapolis.

The Civil War gave Harrison a rare chance to shine, and he emerged a hero and brigadier general, giving him a boost up the ladder of success. His law practice expanded, and he was elected to the U.S. Senate.

The Republicans nominated Harrison for the presidency, and despite rampant

Above: Caroline Scott Harrison lent her prestige as First Lady to many causes, including the Johns Hopkins University Medical School, which she helped on the condition that it admit women. She brought significant renovation to the White House and founded the Daughters of the American Revolution, which commissioned this portrait in her honor.

vote-buying, Harrison lost the popular vote by 90,000. Still, he somehow squeaked to victory in the electoral college. Honest and principled himself, Harrison joined other politicians in allowing business interests to do whatever they wanted. The problems of farmers, workers, and the millions of immigrants streaming into the country were not really of interest to those in power, who cleverly organized things to suit themselves without much input from Harrison.

Right: Benjamin Harrison, the only president to have been the grandson of a previous president, sits at right in the opulent observation car on the presidential train. Both preceded and succeeded by Cleveland, Harrison did virtually nothing to solve the nation's smoldering social and economic problems.

MODERNIZING THE WHITE HOUSE

Carrie was a small, round, white-haired woman, no match in the public's eye for the lovely Frances Cleveland. Still, she spiritedly and publicly set out on a major project—the first ever for a First Lady—improving presidential living conditions. Dismayed by the dilapidated White House, she lobbied for a grandiose rebuilding of the presidential home. Only her husband's failure to court the good will of the Speaker of the House resulted in denial of funding for the project. Carrie then did the next-best thing—with funds allowed for repairs, she spearheaded a complete modernization of the mansion from top to bottom, keeping carpenters, plumbers, painters, and electricians busy for two years.

The White House emerged with a new heating system, new kitchen, new flooring, new bathrooms (previously there had been only one bathroom for the first family!), new curtains, new furniture, and best of all, electric lights (although Carrie was afraid to touch the switches!).

Carrie was not too busy to entertain often, host French classes, paint watercolors, and support women's rights. She is remembered best for discovering leftover china from past presidents stashed away in storerooms and organizing the pieces into an intriguing display which is still admired.

Along with the Harrisons, numerous relatives lived in the White House. Daughter Mamie's little two-year-old, Benjamin Harrison McKee, became the most photographed child ever to live there. "Baby McKee" was stalked by cameramen as he toddled about the south lawn and onto the front pages of the nation's newspapers.

The Harrisons' lives bloomed but briefly in the public eye. Just days before her husband would be defeated in his bid for a second term, Carrie contracted typhoid and died in the White House. Harrison retired but emerged briefly on diplomatic assignments during the McKinley administration. Three years after Carrie's death, he married her niece, Mary Dimmick, who had been Carrie's White House secretary, and at age sixty-four he fathered a baby girl younger than his grandchildren. Mary Harrison outlived her husband by forty-seven years, mistress of the family manors at Indianapolis and in New York State.

Above: *The big bellies of American business bulge over dithering legislators in this 1889 Puck cartoon, "The Bosses of the Senate." Harrison and other politicians essentially let big business interests run the country, ignoring the needs of ordinary people.*

Benjamin Harrison

In Office
Mar. 4, 1889-Mar. 3, 1893
Born Aug. 20, 1833,
North Bend, Ohio
Party: **Republican**

Other Offices:
Brigadier General, 1865
U.S. Senator, 1881-87

Marriages:
Caroline Lavinia Scott Harrison,
1853, married 39 yrs.
Mary Scott Lord Dimmick
Harrison, 1896, married 4 yrs.

Presidential Acts:
Approved costly pension act
for Civil War veterans & their
families.
Approved Sherman Anti-Trust
Act, attempting to control
monopolies.
Approved McKinley Tariff
of 1890, levying controversial
tariffs on imports.
Dealt with crises in Samoa,
Chile, and the Bering Sea.

Died age 67,
Mar. 13, 1901,
Indianapolis, Ind.

Caroline L. S. Harrison

Born Oct. 1, 1832,
Oxford, Ohio
Children:
1 son, 1 daughter

Accomplishments:
Managed home & family during
husband's frequent absences.
First First Lady to oversee large
project; complete overhaul of
White House.
Helped found and supported
DAR and Women's Medical
Fund of Johns Hopkins School
of Medicine.
First First Lady to publicly deliv-
er her own prepared speech.

Died age 60,
Oct. 25, 1892,
Washington, D.C.

WILLIAM MCKINLEY

TWENTY-FIFTH PRESIDENT
1897-1901
IDA SAXTON MCKINLEY

America entered the 20th century under the leadership of William McKinley, a gentleman who was often preoccupied with his ailing wife and who reluctantly commanded U.S. forces to conquer territories of another country.

McKinley began life as one of eight children of an Ohio iron founder, a frail and religious student. He volunteered for duty in the Civil War and was praised for bravery by his commanding

William McKinley

In Office
Mar. 4, 1897-Sept. 14, 1901
Born Jan. 29, 1843, Niles, Ohio
Party: **Republican**

Other Offices:
U.S. Congressman,
1877-83, 1885-91.
Governor of Ohio, 1892-96.

Marriage:
Ida Saxton McKinley, 1871,
married 30 yrs.

Presidential Acts:
Focused on difficult tariff issues.
Presided over War with Spain,
gaining Cuban independence,
American dominion over
Puerto Rico, the Philippines,
and Guam.
Annexed Hawaii.
Sent expedition to China
during Boxer Rebellion.

Died age 58,
Sept. 14, 1901,
Buffalo, N.Y.

Right: William McKinley guided America out of the old century and into the new. He was the last president to have been a Civil War veteran. Mannerly and devoted to caring for his ailing wife, McKinley reluctantly presided over the country's most brash imperialistic adventurism—its conflict with Spain.

officer, Rutherford B. Hayes. Promoted to Major at twenty-two, he returned home to study law and set up practice in Canton, Ohio. Handsome and winning, his political career took him to Congress and to two terms as Ohio's Governor.

Left: With American interests in Cuba threatened, and the United States Navy well prepared, war was declared on Spain. At the Battle of Santiago Bay, Cuba, July 3, 1898, pictured above, American ships trapped and destroyed a Spanish fleet. By August, the United States had taken control of the Philippines, Guam, and Puerto Rico and won independence for Cuba.

IN SICKNESS AND IN HEALTH

As a young major, William caught the eye of beautiful well-educated Ida Saxton. Ida's cameo face brightened her father's bank, where she was learning finance. Soon Ida could scarcely bear for William to be apart from her for even a moment—an augur of the years to come. Upon their marriage, Banker Saxton gave his daughter a fine home—but apparently he could not give her good health.

The idyll of the early days of the McKinleys' marriage was shattered by the deaths of their two tiny daughters and Ida's plunge into illness. Medical records are incomplete, but Ida apparently spent most of her married life suffering from epilepsy and semi-infantile behavior, drugged by barbituates and other prescriptions. Her husband catered to her every whim and virtually never left her side for more than an hour at a time.

Backed by the Republican party, especially millionaire industrialist Mark Hanna, McKinley easily won election to the presidency. At the inaugural ball, Ida proudly promenaded in white satin and diamonds—her favorite jewels—and suddenly fell down unconscious. Before the amazed crowds, the President calmly carried her from the room. Ida delighted in attending many official functions, and each time she suffered a seizure, McKinley covered her face with a handkerchief to reduce embarrassment.

Arguments over gold and silver monetary standards and tariffs dominated domestic politics, while the Spanish-American War led to America confidently moving into a dominant position on the global stage.

THE BELOVED INVALID

As his cabinet discussed weighty matters of international import, the President was often called to his wife's side to calm her tantrums or to bring her a needle, a pen, or a book. She diligently crocheted thousands of bedroom slippers, which she donated to friends and charities. The White House staff competently carried out its duties without her guidance, since she refused to allow anyone else to act as hostess. Although she sometimes seemed imbecilic, Ida had strong opinions on some things, including the need to Christianize the people of the Philippines—a policy she urged on the president, influencing his decision to retain the Islands.

National prosperity eased McKinley into a second term, and he and Ida went on tour and enjoyed a vacation. They halted at Buffalo to visit the Pan-American Exposition, where the President unwisely mingled with the milling crowds. An anarchist, Leon Czolgosz, pushed forward with a pistol draped with a handkerchief and shot twice.

The President took eight days to die. In his gangrenous fever, McKinley put his arm around Ida and feebly recited, "Nearer My God to Thee"—his last words. The bereft widow bore up through the state funeral and six subsequent years with surprising strength, never again suffering an attack of the illness that kept her husband so close to her side for over three decades.

Ida Saxton McKinley

Born Jun. 8, 1847, Canton, Ohio
Children: 2 daughters
(died young)

Accomplishments:
Worked in banking before marriage.
Crocheted thousands of slippers for donations.

Died age 59, May 26, 1907, Canton, Ohio

Below: Ida Saxton McKinley mystified those around her with her strange behavior. Once beautiful and vivacious, she became an invalid almost parasitic on her husband. McKinley's assassination, tragic though it was, seemed almost to give her the strength to live slightly more independently than when he was attending to her every whim.

THEODORE ROOSEVELT

TWENTY-SIXTH PRESIDENT
1901-1909
EDITH CAROW ROOSEVELT

As President McKinley's life ebbed away in Buffalo, New York, where he had been shot, Vice President Theodore Roosevelt was climbing a peak in the Adirondacks. An urgent message brought him down the treacherous slopes in the dark to catch a special train to Buffalo, where he hastily took the oath of office—and began a new phase in the American presidency.

A man of extraordinary derring-do and physicality, Roosevelt enthusiastically grasped the helm of a nation taking the center of the world stage. Brash, bright, verbal, and dynamic, T.R., as he came to be called, made the presidency stronger than ever before, which he considered appropriate for a strong and energetic country. In the seven-and-a-half years of his presidency, T.R. changed the notion of president from that of a genteel leader willing to let business interests gouge the citizenry to that of an activist seeking to promote the interests of ordinary people and save the environment from untrammeled destruction. Born into a wealthy New York family, he was completely at ease being treated almost like royalty, even as he championed the underdog and the common good.

Edith Roosevelt, T.R.'s First Lady, daughter of New York gentry, was similarly accustomed to privilege, and she brought a graceful yet firm guiding hand to a panoply of White House events previously unequalled in American history, while at the same time raising six lively offspring.

POLITICAL BEGINNINGS

Roosevelt was called "Teedie" as a child and was not nicknamed "Teddy" until later. He was a sickly, asthmatic boy who as a youth sprang into action, built up his body, and became extremely tough. He took up boxing at Harvard, where he was an excellent student. He married delightful Alice Lee, like himself a member of a well-placed family, and attended Columbia Law School, seeking diversion by riding horseback through Central Park and even scaling the Matterhorn. Elected to the New York Assembly, he charged financier Jay Gould with attempting to corrupt a judge, noting that Gould was "part of that most dangerous of all dangerous classes, the wealthy criminal class." This would be T.R.'s theme throughout his political career.

Valentine's Day, 1884, brought tragedy to T.R.—both his mother and his young wife died that day, victims of typhoid and a post-partum infection. Roosevelt left his newborn daughter, Alice, with his domineering sister Anna, and headed for two years of rough ranch life in the Badlands. Upon his return to New York, he married his childhood

Theodore Roosevelt

In Office Sept. 14,1901-Mar.3, 1909
Born Oct. 27, 1858, New York, N.Y.
Party: Republican

Other Offices:
N Y State Assemblyman, 1882-84.
Member, U.S. Civil Service Commission, 1889-95.
President, New York City Board of Police Commissioners, 1895.
Assistant Secretary of the Navy, 1897-98.
Organizer of first regiment U.S. volunteer cavalry—"Roosevelt's Rough Riders", 1898.
Governor of New York, 1899-1901.
Vice President, 1901.

Marriages:
Alice Hathaway Lee Roosevelt, 1880, married 3 yrs., l daughter
(Born 1861, Died 1884)
Edith K. Carow Roosevelt, 1886, married 32 yrs.

Presidential Acts:
Fought monopolies with strengthened Sherman Antitrust Act of 1890.
Upheld striking United Mine Workers, 1902.
Established Dept. of Commerce & Labor to increase industrial growth and improve working conditions.
Preserved millions of acres of land for public use.
Enhanced U.S. power through Panama Canal construction.
Issued Roosevelt Corollary to the Monroe Doctrine, 1904, warning against foreign intervention in the Western Hemisphere.
Settled Alaska border dispute with Canada.
Signed the Pure Food and Drug Act, 1906.
Won Nobel Peace Prize for ending Russian-Japanese conflict, 1906.

Died age 60, Jan. 6, 1919,
Oyster Bay, N.Y.

Left: *Theodore Roosevelt firmly grasped the reins of power as president of a vibrant nation. Not quite forty-three, the youngest man ever to accede to the presidency, he made the office stronger than ever before. His crusades for reform, though flawed, were unprecented, backing the people's cries for justice and decency. He used the White House as a "bully pulpit" from which to expound his ideas of right and power.*

Left: *Cutting the Panama Canal through Central America was made possible by a flagrant episode of imperialism masterminded by Roosevelt. The challenging project, begun in 1906 and not finished until 1914, enhanced U.S. power on both the Atlantic and the Pacific. Hampered by yellow fever, bubonic plague, and sliding volcanic rocks, the canal cost $380 million and many lives.*

Above: *Edith Carow Roosevelt brought admirable energy and traditional elite values to her task as national hostess and manager of a fun-loving family. Serenely posed on the south grounds of the mansion in this portrait, Edith approved plans for a complete White House rebuilding, including a new entryway corridor displaying likenesses of First Ladies. Her husband respected her strength; she was the only person who could control him.*

sweetheart, Edith Carow, who reared Alice and bore him five more children.

As he rose in politics, T.R. gained national attention for vociferously fighting corruption and supporting good causes, such as limits on child labor. He was also a frank advocate of imperialistic territorial conquest, viewing it as a mark of superiority of the strong over the weak.

He rushed to fight in the Spanish-American War, whipping a band of macho cavalry volunteers into shape as the renowned "Rough Riders," leading them in a famous charge up Cuba's San Juan Hill. T.R. returned a hero—and soon became New York Governor, Vice President and then President. In keeping with his nice tough-guy image was his slogan, a West African proverb, "Speak softly and carry a big stick."

DYNAMIC LEADERSHIP

The match between the mood of the nation and the new president was perfect. It was a time of dramatic social and economic ferment, with a burgeoning progessive movement demanding an end to capitalistic abuses and to the plundering of the nation's ecological resources. T.R. lent the tremendous prestige of a newly-powerful presidency to the progressive movement, striking out against the tyranny of wealth. He moved against illegal trusts, supported the striking United Mine Workers, and pursued the "Square Deal," a series of domestic reforms. Conservation was a favorite cause—he established fifty game preserves and doubled the number of national parks.

Roosevelt realized that building the Panama Canal would increase U.S. power in both the Atlantic and the Pacific, and when he met opposition from Colombia, which owned the isthmus, T.R. openly encouraged Panama to declare independence. The agreeable leaders of the revolt collected their profits, and the U.S. had its Canal Zone.

Immensely popular, Roosevelt earned the endearing nickname "Teddy" when he refused to shoot a bear cub, inspiring the Teddy bear toy loved by Americans ever since. He loved to romp with his children, tramp on fifty-mile hikes, write books, and hog the limelight.

For arbitrating an end to the Russo-Japanese War, Roosevelt won the Nobel Peace Prize. He also sought to keep peace in Asia by ostentatiously sending the battle fleet of the U.S. Navy on a world cruise to impress Japan with American strength.

A SPIRITED FAMILY

The Roosevelt White House was like a circus. The children dragged many pets—even a pony—through the presidential portals, frolicked on the lawn and in the potted palms, and kept Edith hopping when she was not organizing one of her endless entertainments—elaborate receptions, teas, parties, dinners, dances, and breakfasts. Entertaining became part of a wider scheme to promote the glory of the presidency and thus America's new world power. The sagging White House was completely modernized and redecorated under Edith's direction—almost obliterating history but bringing the mansion in line with the needs of a twentieth-century presidential family.

Edith carefully pruned her guest lists, using Cabinet wives as sources of gossip to cut anyone deemed guilty of social or moral offense. Though her husband invited the eminent black educator Booker T. Washington to dine, Edith excluded African American women from her events.

Capturing the public imagination was daughter Alice, a vivacious rebel, who kept a garter snake in her purse, flaunted her cigarettes, and drove about in her own car. She was an idol to women around the world, and her favorite color, a particular blue-gray, was dubbed "Alice blue." Thousands of bolts of fabric were dyed this hue, and the hit song "Alice Blue Gown" swept the country. Alice's 1906 White House wedding to Nicholas Longworth was a gala spectacle. Hundreds of selected guests witnessed the ceremony in the East Room, adorned with garlands of Easter lilies. The bride carried orchids—and sliced the wedding cake with a borrowed sword.

In 1909, T.R. handed William Howard Taft the presidency and zoomed off to Africa to bag five hundred animals on a Smithsonian-sponsored expedition. Back in New York, he was greeted by an enormous Fifth Avenue parade, considered retirement, but then again sought the presidency—unsuccessfully. He was shot while campaigning but delivered his speech anyway, with a bullet in his chest. He later survived a dangerous Amazon expedition. Finally, the death of his son Quentin during World War I and a coronary occlusion killed him at just sixty. Edith lived until age eighty-seven, engaged in traveling, reading, and charity work.

Left: Hunting trophies and memorabilia decorate the North Room at Sagamore Hill, the Roosevelt family's beloved estate at Oyster Bay, Long Island, New York. The first president to journey outside the country while in office and an experienced world traveler, T.R. loved his home at Sagamore Hill more deeply than any place on earth. Intended for Roosevelt's first bride, the estate and its lively family life was run by his second wife, elegant Edith.

Left: Grimacing T.R. heads leer from every side in a 1909 Puck cartoon ridiculing the heavy Roosevelt hand on every aspect of the presidency. Roosevelt's successor, William Howard Taft, lurching through the door, is shocked by what he sees. Under Roosevelt, the White House underwent extreme change, both in the mansion itself and in the way presidential power was used.

William Howard Taft

In Office
Mar. 4, 1909-Mar. 3, 1913
Born Sept. 15, 1857,
Cincinnati, Ohio
***Party:* Republican**

Other Offices:
Superior Court Judge,
Cincinnati, 1887-90.
U.S. Solicitor General, 1890-92.
Judge, U.S. Circuit Court,
1892-1900.
President, Philippines
Commission, 1900-01.
Governor General, Philippine
Islands, 1901-04.
Secretary of War, 1904-08.
Chief Justice, U.S. Supreme
Court, 1913-21.

Marriage:
Helen Herron Taft, 1886,
married 43 yrs.

Presidential Acts:
Helped enact Sixteenth
Amendment to the Constitution,
providing Federal authority to
levy income taxes, 1909-13.
Oversaw Payne-Aldrich
Tariff Bill, 1909.
Supported efforts to weaken
monopolies.
Helped enact Seventeenth
Amendment to the Constitution,
providing for popular election
of senators, 1912-13.
Enacted numerous governmental
reforms, reducing corruption.
Supported laws aiding environ-
mental conservation.

Died age 72, Mar. 8, 1930,
Washington, D.C.

WILLIAM HOWARD TAFT

TWENTY-SEVENTH
PRESIDENT
1909-1913
HELEN HERRON TAFT

William Howard Taft's wife Nellie wanted him to become President of the United States. He obliged her—and then went on to do what he wanted to do—become Chief Justice of the Supreme Court.

One of six surviving children of a prominent jurist in Cincinnati, Ohio, Taft excelled at Yale and returned to his home town to practice law. Physically large, witty, and humorous, he rose to a judgeship and was chosen to be U.S. Solicitor General under President Harrison. In Washington, he met young Theodore Roosevelt, and the two became fast friends.

While at a sledding party in Cincinnati, Taft offered a ride on his bobsled to a young socialite, Helen (Nellie) Herron. They coursed down the slopes to eventual marriage, honeymooned in Britain, and settled into domesticity, eventually rearing three successful children. They were devoted to one another throughout their marriage.

A WIFE'S AMBITION

When Taft took his wedding vows, he may not have realized that he was pledging himself to fulfill his wife's ambitions. She grew up in Cincinnati, gazing across the street at a mansion designed by White House architect James Hoban, only slightly less imposing than the actual Executive Mansion. As a girl of sixteen, Nellie had been invited to the White House itself by her father's former law partner, President Hayes. "Nothing in my life reaches the climax of human bliss I felt when...I was entertained at the White House," Nellie recalled. Her goal was formed: return to the mansion not as a guest but as First Lady.

Throughout their marriage, Nellie guided Taft toward positions she believed would lead to 1600 Pennsylvania Avenue. In this she echoed Taft's father, who also held this ambition for his son. Taft genially went along with the plan.

Taft was selected for more significant judiciary posts, and then was sent to Manila as Governor General to carry out U.S. policies in the Philippines. Nellie delighted in their years in the tropics, particularly enjoying her reign at the opulent Malacanan Palace, where thousands of Filipinos sometimes rallied in praise of Taft.

President Teddy Roosevelt personally offered Taft a choice of either a Supreme Court appointment or a presidential candidacy. The first was Taft's true desire—but he agreed to the latter, in deference to his wife's wishes. With Roosevelt's backing, Taft easily won election.

THE RELUCTANT PRESIDENT

When Taft rode from the inaugural to the White House, his wife sat beside him in the carriage—a precedent-setting first for a presidential partner. On the threshhold of the White House, she gazed enthralled at the presidential seal set in the floor, thrilled that at last her goal had been realized. For the inaugural ball, she wore a heavy white satin gown exquisitely embroidered in Japan in a goldenrod pattern—one detail among many that she arranged.

President Taft struggled with a multitude of national problems, many well beyond his political abilities to solve. Failures in international diplomacy, however, were counterbalanced by domestic successes—he lowered tariffs, initiated twice as many anti-trust lawsuits as had Roosevelt, strengthened the Interstate Commerce Commission, placed conservation efforts on a strong legal footing, and attacked corruption.

Nellie focused on garden parties and many other entertainments, always a perfectionist. An unfortunate stroke sidelined her for a year, while her daughter and sisters performed official duties. An event still unequalled was the Tafts' magnificent 1911 silver wedding anniversary party, where 8,000 guests mingled beneath multicolored lights glittering all over the White House and its grounds.

Temperamental Roosevelt ended up attacking his protege, and ran against him in the 1912 election, thus dividing the Republican vote and ensuring Woodrow Wilson's victory. Taft was delighted to leave his difficult White House job, and moved to a law professorship at Yale. He worked to create a world peace organization, and finally, under President Harding, was selected Chief Justice of the Supreme Court, a post he contentedly held for eight years. After his death in 1930, Nellie lived on another thirteen years and was buried beside her husband in Arlington National Cemetery, the first presidential wife to be interred there.

Helen Herron Taft

**Born Jan. 2, 1861,
Cincinnati, Ohio
Children: 2 sons, 1 daughter**

Accomplishments:
**Reared three accomplished children.
Actively aided her husband's career.
Arranged planting of Washington cherry trees.
First President's wife to see her book published commercially,
Recollections of Full Years,
1914.**

**Died age 82,
May 22, 1943,
Washington, D.C.**

Below: Intelligent Helen (Nellie) Herron Taft was spurred by presidential ambitions much of her life—not for herself but for her husband. She urged Taft to accept positions likely to lead to the presidency and entertained lavishly to help him gain name recognition. She organized a gala silver wedding anniversary party more glittering than all other White House festivities.

Above: *Perhaps the most lasting memento of the Taft administration is the splendid display of cherry blossoms which beautifies the capital each spring. The planting of thousands of Japanese cherry trees was arranged by Nellie Taft, aided by gifts of trees sent by the Mayor of Tokyo. The glorious blooms are an annual delight.*

WOODROW WILSON

TWENTY-EIGHTH PRESIDENT
1913-1921
ELLEN AXSON WILSON
EDITH GALT WILSON

Woodrow Wilson was president in a time of great trial for the United States and for the world. A scholarly man of principle, devoted to the cause of world peace, he was fortunate to have had the loving support of two intelligent and deeply caring women.

FIRM FOUNDATIONS

Son of a distinguished Presbyterian minister, he spent a frail childhood surrounded by discussions of high ideals. He was born in Virginia, moved to Georgia and South Carolina, and attended college at Princeton, New Jersey. There, and in law school at the University of Virginia, he honed his talents as a persuasive speaker and author, publishing his first book, *Congressional Government*. An academic career followed, leading him to become president of Princeton University. Elected governor of New Jersey, Wilson chalked up a highly successful record of reform, which led to the Democratic nomination and election to the presidency.

Wilson's lovely wife Ellen embodied the finest virtues of the Southern woman. Georgia-born, her father also a Presbyterian minister, she was known for her ability to create an extremely warm and inviting home environment for her three daughters and a multitude of guests. She enjoyed painting, but her true gift was nurturing her family and friends in a series of modest dwellings and fine homes. She also proof-read her husband's writings and speeches. The Wilsons' marriage was very loving; it is said that they never quarreled in their three decades together.

THE FIRST TERM

At the White House, Ellen, or Nell, as she was called, worked with the professional Executive Mansion staff to arrange a round of entertainments. Two of the Wilsons' gracious daughters married in formal White House weddings. Deeply interested in better housing for the poor Black population of Washington, Nell led congressmen through filthy alleyways and persuaded them to provide legislative support for a housing program. Sadly, Nell's life was shortened by kidney trouble, and she died in 1914, five days after war broke out in Europe. Wilson was miserable, and the White House was plunged into gloom.

During his first term Wilson prodded Congress to revise the banking and loan system, establish a farmers' credit system, strengthen anti-trust laws, revise tariffs and income taxes, and pass laws protecting labor. He unwillingly allowed American intervention in the Mexican Revolution, but he averted war with Mexico. As Wilson's second term began, the tragedies of

Right: American pilots who volunteered to serve in the French army before 1917 formed an organization called the Lafayette Escadrille, shown here bombing a German airfield. During World War I, both sides used airplanes for large-scale fighting, and air battles became common.

Right: Woodrow Wilson was an independent thinker, devoted to seeking world peace. However, World War I and the failure of the United States Senate to join the League of Nations, precourser of the United Nations, brought him deep disappointment.

Below: The gallantry of American naval forces is emphasized in this 1918 poster urging purchase of Liberty bonds to support the war effort. Despite years of warning, the United States was ill-prepared for full-scale participation in the war and hastily instituted measures to finance the war and fill military ranks.

World War I dominated the news, and the primary question concerning the nation was whether or not the United States would get involved.

WORLD WAR

High-minded Wilson maintained American neutrality and strove mightily to keep the nation out of the European conflagration, but the Germans almost dared him to declare war. A German U-boat sank the *Lusitania* in 1915, killing 1,198 men, women, and children, including 128 Americans, and in 1917 announced they planned to continue such aggression. More merchant ships were sunk, and bowing to public pressure, Wilson asked Congress to declare war on Germany in April of 1917. War fever swept the country, and all thoughts and efforts turned toward defeating the aggressors.

INVEST IN TI
VICTORY LIBERTY

In the meantime, the President had met and fallen in love with Edith Galt, the widow of a prosperous Washington jeweler, who had grown up as the daughter of a Virginia lawyer and judge. Proud of her heritage as a descendent of Pocahontas and John Rolfe, fashionable Edith was famous in the capital as the only woman driving her own electric car about town. Isolated and lonely in his lofty leadership, Woodrow persuaded her to be his wife, and they were married sixteen months after Nell had died. Edith immediately reinstated affection and a strong womanly presence in the presidential home.

With American men dying in Europe, Edith stopped all official entertaining and began to sew pajamas and shirts for the Red Cross. She joined other government ladies in serving military men at a Washington Red Cross canteen, and the president sometimes stopped by to talk to the men before they shipped out.

THEY KEPT THE SEA LANES OPEN

THE W.P. POWERS CO. LITHO, N.Y.

E LOAN

AN IMPERFECT PEACE

Wilson prepared for peace by formulating his Fourteen Points, calling for forgiveness of the vanquished, open relationships between countries, disarmament, and a League of Nations. Shortly after the armistice ended the war, he and Edith sailed for Europe. At Versailles, Wilson joined other heads of state to pound out the final terms of the peace. Rejecting Wilson's idealism, the other leaders insisted on imposing the harshest terms on Germany, thereby sowing the seeds of World War II.

At home, Wilson fought a hard fight to have his League of Nations approved by the Senate, traveling ten thousand miles cross-country to appeal to the American people. Wilson collapsed with a paralytic stroke, and while he was ill, his project for peace was rejected by the Senate. For his efforts, however, he won the Nobel Peace Prize.

During the months of Wilson's illness, he was a recluse in his White House bedroom. Edith scarcely left his side, screening visitors, tabling issues of lesser importance, and ferrying messages to and fro, thus enabling the president to continue in office without the public being fully aware of his disabilities. For playing this role, Edith has been called the "First Woman President." Although Edith's influence was extremely strong, there is evidence that Wilson remained in control of major decisions.

Wilson's health ultimately improved, and he was able to escort his successor, Warren G. Harding, to the Capitol for his inauguration. He and Edith moved to a house in Washington, where crowds often gathered to pay tribute to the man who gave his utmost in the cause of world peace. Within three years, he passed away. Edith lived on to see six more presidents, and died in 1961, on the eve of the anniversary of Woodrow Wilson's birth.

Ellen Louise Axson Wilson

Born May 15, 1860, Savannah, Ga.
Children: **3 daughters**

Accomplishments:
Created nurturing home for her children and husband, enabling his professorial and political accomplishments. Worked for slum improvement.

Died age 54, Aug. 6, 1914, Washington, D.C.

Edith Bolling Galt Wilson

Born Oct. 15, 1872, Wytheville, Va.
Children: **none**

Accomplishments:
Successfully managed first husband's jewelry business after his death. Supported president during difficult times. Was virtual Acting President, 1919-20.

Died age 89, Dec. 28, 1961, Washington, D.C.

Right: *Edith Galt Wilson, a widow, met and married President Wilson after his first wife died. In her mid-forties at the time this portrait was painted, shortly after her marriage to Wilson, Edith was an ardent supporter of her uncompromising husband and was criticized for exercising considerable power during his long illness.*

WARREN G. HARDING

TWENTY-NINTH PRESIDENT
1921-1923
FLORENCE KLING HARDING

Warren G. Harding did not seem destined for greatness, lacking as he was in great intellect or political accomplishment. He was, however, charming and good-looking. At least one politician who backed him for the presidency said he did so because he "looked like a President." His administration is historically significant primarily because of the scandals it generated. While

Right: Handsome Warren G. Harding looked the part of a President, but he himself admitted, "I knew that this job would be too much for me." Confused by governmental complexities, he was unable to stop his shrewd colleagues from raking in illegal profits. As a Senator, he voted for Prohibition—but as President, he served drinks at White House poker parties.

Warren Gamaliel Harding

In Office Mar.4, 1921-Aug. 2, 1923
Born Nov. 2, 1865, Corsica, Ohio
Party: **Republican**

Other Offices:
Ohio State Senator, 1899-1903.
Ohio Lt. Governor, 1904-5.
U.S. Senator, 1915-21.

Marriage:
Florence K. Harding, 1891, married 32 yrs.

Presidential Acts:
Supported Fordney-McCumber Tariff Act, 1922.
Oversaw Washington Disarmament Conference involving the great powers, 1921-22.
Failed to control corruption of many in his administration, especially the Teapot Dome scandal.

Died age 57, Aug. 2, 1923, San Francisco, Calif.

Harding himself was not implicated, the wrongdoing occured on his watch and contributed to his sudden death.

WINNING WAYS

Oldest of eight children of an Ohio farmer who became a doctor, young Harding finished school at a tiny college and wound up in the newspaper business. At age nineteen, he and two partners purchased the small Marion *Star* for $300, and Harding made it a success. In the small town of Marion, he met his future wife, Florence, a strong-willed woman who would accompany him on his unexpected rise to the White House.

Florence, the daughter of a conservative Mennonite hardware store owner in Marion, rejected the simple life and at age nineteen eloped with a ne'er-do-well who deserted her and her small son. Florence managed to support herself and her child by giving piano lessons to neighborhood children. She divorced her husband, and he died soon afterward. When handsome Harding came to town, Florence was interested, even though he was five years her junior. After they wed, she took over the newspaper's circulation department, running it with an iron hand. Her husband called her "the Duchess."

Harding's flair for public speaking and friendly hand-shaking helped him move up the political ladder from local to state and national levels. His election as U.S. Senator seemed the apogee of his career, and he and Florence enjoyed partying in Washington society for several years. One of their more affluent friends often wore her favorite gem—the Hope Diamond. Affable Harding became known as someone more crafty politicians could control, and this led to his presidential nomination.

In the wake of the disappointing Wilson years, the public chose Harding as president, little suspecting that what they were getting was a charming puppet of nefarious interests. His womanizing and fathering a child out of wedlock did not become publicly known until after his death.

HINTS OF SCANDAL

Once in the Executive Mansion, the Hardings entertained often, fully utilizing the competent services of the permanent White House staff. Florence opened the mansion and grounds to the public, and organized regular garden parties for veterans, despite her own ill health. The Hardings held private poker parties several times a week, serving what was contraband alcohol in those Prohibition years. Attending these get-togethers were many so-called friends, officials who were deeply involved in graft and theft.

Word began to reach the President of some of these scandalous activities, and he worried about whether or not to expose his political cronies. Ill with heart disease, he began a political tour of Alaska and the West. He and Florence traveled by special train, stopping for speeches and informal appearances before approving crowds. Collapsing into a suite at the Palace Hotel in San Francisco, he died.

Suddenly, skeletons started tumbling out of closets, and scandalmongers even accused Florence of poisoning her husband. In truth, she was devoted to him, ineffectual though he was in controlling his scheming colleagues. She stalwartly accompanied his funeral train as it moved across the country past crowds of mourners, and she participated in the state funeral. Ill herself, she tried to salvage her husband's honor by destroying as much of his correspondence as she could. She died in Marion scarcely more than a year after his death.

Below: "The Duchess" to her husband, Florence Harding had been a small-town teenage rebel. Through hard work and careful management, she was able to take herself and her gregarious husband to the White House. She was hostess at wine-free state dinners, and personally poured more potent drinks at private presidential gatherings.

Florence Kling De Wolfe Harding

Born Aug. 15, 1860, Marion, Ohio
Children: **1 son by first husband**

Accomplishments:
Worked as music teacher, helped husband in newspaper business. Helped orchestrate her husband's rise to the presidency.

**Died age 64,
Nov. 21, 1924, Marion, Ohio**

Left: After Harding's demise, the full scope of the graft which had burgeoned during his administration came to light. Most spectacular was the scandal of the leasing of the Teapot Dome oil reserve in Wyoming to private interests who paid Secretary of the Interior Albert Fall $125,000 in kickbacks. Other shady deals involved the Secretary of the Navy, the Veterans Bureau chief, and the Attorney General.

CALVIN COOLIDGE

THIRTIETH PRESIDENT
1923-1929
GRACE GOODHUE COOLIDGE

His campaign stickers said, "Keep Cool with Coolidge for President," but "cool" is hardly a word associated with President Coolidge these days; "colorless" is more like it. Lacking in charisma and flamboyancy, "Silent Cal" is remembered for his dry Yankee wit and extreme frugality with words. His administration was rather uneventful, but Coolidge did demonstrate determination to restore dignity and morality to the highest office in the land. He was associated with good times called "Coolidge prosperity"—a period of blissful ignorance of the Crash and Depression to come.

SHYNESS AND CHARM
Coolidge grew up thrifty, sensible, and shy in an isolated Vermont farm hamlet, raised by his storekeeper father and homemaker mother who died young. He studied at Amherst and took up law and politics—perhaps a strange choice for an introvert with an expressionless face. He was always restrained and correct, even when wooing a vivacious young woman, Grace Goodhue, whom he had seen in the precincts of the Clarke School for the Deaf where he had rented a room (though neither was deaf).

Grace was the only child of conservative parents who encouraged her activities in church and school. She loved ice skating, picnics, and boat excursions, and at the University of Vermont, she founded a chapter of Pi Beta Phi sorority. After college, she began teaching at the Clarke School, where she found herself drawn to her shy suitor, even though he completely lacked romantic imagination. They were wed on a rainy fall day, the bride clad in a gray dress, and traveled to Montreal for their honeymoon.

For years they lived in a rented duplex for $27 a month, sticking to Coolidge's parsimonious ways. Their two sons grew as Coolidge held a variety of local and state offices. Grace indeed embodied her name, pleasantly accepting her husband's silences, business-related absences, and unwillingness to consult her on anything important.

Calvin Coolidge

In Office Aug.3, 1923-Mar. 3, 1929
Born July 4, 1872, Plymouth, Vt.
Party: **Republican**

Other Offices:
City Councilman, Northampton, Mass., 1899.
City Solicitor, Court Clerk, Northampton, 1900-1904.
Massachusetts State Representative, 1907-08.
Mayor, Northampton, 1910-11.
Massachusetts State Senator, 1912-15.
Massachusetts Lt. Governor, 1916-18.
Massachusetts Governor, 1919-20.
Vice President, 1921-23.

Marriage:
Grace Goodhue Coolidge, 1905, married 27 yrs.

Presidential Acts:
Vetoed Adjusted Compensation Act benefiting veterans, (veto overridden) 1924.
Participated in Kellogg-Briand Peace Pact renouncing war, 1928.
Vetoed measures to help farmers.
Opposed restrictions on Japanese immigration, (Veto overridden) 1924.
Improved relations with Mexico.

Died age 60, Jan. 5, 1933, Northampton, Mass.

Left: Alice White plays a campus cutie dancing the Charleston atop a grand piano in the 1929 movie "Hot Stuff," directed by Mervyn LeRoy. Short skirts, new roles for women, radios, record players, movies, cars, telephones, and a multitude of other technological and social innovations were altering the face of America as Coolidge stepped down, ending an era.

SUDDENLY PRESIDENT

Selected as Harding's vice president, Coolidge and his family moved to Washington, where Grace glowed in lovely new clothing, and her good disposition became an important social asset to her sphinx-like husband. They were visiting Vermont when a nighttime telegram informed them of Harding's death. By the warm light of kerosene lamps, Coolidge was sworn in as President by his father, a notary public. This homey scene, portrayed later in articles and paintings, endeared the awkward new president to the American people.

Coolidge had already achieved some fame, when, as Massachusetts Governor, he had quelled riots resulting from a policemen's strike in Boston. As president his philosophy was certainly not an interventionist one: he essentially believed in leaving things alone as much as possible. He let American prosperity take its course, which looked like a good one, until just after Coolidge left office.

The new occupants of the White House lived decorously, following Prohibition laws, allowing endless press photographs of themselves, their teenaged sons, and their many pets— white collies, cats, a raccoon, and several canaries. Grace was a proper and friendly hostess, and even the President displayed improved social skills.

Tragedy beset the family—while playing tennis, young Calvin got a blister on his foot which became fatally infected. Grace later published a touching poem about the loss of her sixteen-year-old son, including the lines:

Your kiss upon my cheek
Has made me feel the gentle touch
Of Him who leads us on.
The memory of your smile,
*   when young,*
Reveals His face....

Coolidge wrote sadly, "I do not know why such a price was exacted for occupying the White House." Despite his dull exterior, he often felt deep, yet concealed, emotions.

Coolidge was elected in his own right in 1924, but he declined to run again in 1928. He and Grace retired to Northampton, where he wrote his autobiography and newspaper articles. He lived to see economic disaster strike the nation and died just two months before Franklin Roosevelt and the Democrats took over Washington in 1933. Grace was left with some $700,000, which she used for European travel and living comfortably for many years. She kept in touch with her sorority friends and raised funds for the Clarke School, where she had first met her stiff but idealistic husband.

Grace Anna Goodhue Coolidge

Born Jan. 3, 1879, Burlington, Vt.
***Children:* 2 sons**

Accomplishments:
Founded college sorority chapter.
Taught at and raised funds for the Clarke School for the Deaf, Northampton.
Graciously coordinated family and White House events.

Died age 78, July 8, 1957, Northampton, Mass.

Left: Grace Goodhue Coolidge lived up to her name, gracefully providing support and a warm life for her husband and family. John F. Kennedy, who knew her in her latter years when both were trustees at the Clarke School in Massachusetts, said she epitomized "the qualities of graciousness, charm and modesty which marked her as an ideal First Lady of the Land." In this White House portrait, she appears with her white collie, Rob Roy.

Right: *A true humanitarian and believer in the ability of Americans to prosper through hard work, Herbert Hoover failed to conquer the massive economic forces of Depression that gripped the country during his administration. Optimistically declaring that "prosperity is just around the corner," Hoover hoped to lead the nation to victory over poverty but instead presided over economic debacle.*

Herbert Clark Hoover

In Office Mar. 4, 1929-Mar. 3, 1933
Born Aug. 10, 1874, West Branch, Iowa
***Party:* Republican**

Other Offices:
Chairman, American Relief Committee, London, 1914-15.
Chairman, Commission for Relief, Belgium, 1915-18.
U.S. Food Administrator, 1917-19.
Chairman, European Relief Council, 1920.
Secretary of Commerce, 1921-28.
Coordinator, European Food Program, 1946.
Chairman, Hoover Commission on Administrative Reform, 1947-49, 1953-55.

Marriage:
Lou Henry Hoover, 1899, married 44 yrs.

Presidential Acts:
Approved Hawley-Smoot Tariff, raising trade barriers, 1930.
Vetoed Norris bill to aid unemployed, 1931.
Authorized attack on Bonus Army march to Washington, 1932.
Created Reconstruction Finance Corp. to aid industry, 1932.

Died age 90, Oct. 20, 1964, New York, N.Y.

HERBERT HOOVER

THIRTY-FIRST PRESIDENT 1929-1933

LOU HENRY HOOVER

Herbert Hoover achieved eminence in three fields—mining engineering, administering humanitarian relief, and politics. In the first two he received unqualifiedly high marks, but in the third his marks were poor. Whether or not he truly deserved as much criticism as he received is a matter of debate, but the fact is that his name became virtually a synonym for hard times in America.

Closely bonded to Hoover was his wife Lou, to whom he was married for forty-four years, through days of glory and of difficulty. Their bright minds sparked off each other and enhanced their time together.

POVERTY TO RICHES

He was born in Iowa, the son of a poor Quaker blacksmith who died when the boy was a toddler. His mother supported her three children by taking in sewing, but she too died, and the children were parceled out to various relatives. Herbert went to live with a teacher uncle in Oregon, and later worked his way through Stanford University in Palo Alto, California, where he earned a degree in mining engineering.

With no better job available, he did manual labor in a gold mine for $2 a day and felt despair when he got laid off. Despite these experiences, he eventually accumulated a fortune of some four million dollars, and as President, treated desperate unemployed demonstrators harshly. He was a firm believer in personal industry and public service, but sometimes his application of these ideas seemed unsympathetic to people in dire straits.

Hoover met his bride-to-be in a geology lab at Stanford. A banker's daughter, lithe Lou was an active lover of outdoor adventures and a seeker of interesting experiences. Like Hoover, she was an Iowan transplanted to the West Coast. They dated, corresponded, and then married when Hoover got his first good job. A day after their wedding, they were off for China, where Hoover began work as technical manager of the Chinese Engineering and Mining Company. Part of his job was prospecting for gold in the Gobi Desert.

WORKING AROUND THE WORLD

Their years abroad included exciting stays in China, torn by the Boxer Rebellion; Burma, where Hoover was busy earning money with fabulous silver mines; and London, where they lived in high style, punctuated by visits to Palo Alto, where their two sons attended school for a while.

They were in London when World War I erupted, and Hoover became a civilian hero organizing food relief for millions of starving Belgians while Lou rolled up her sleeves for the British war effort. Hoover was brought to Washington as Wilson's Food Administrator, sent to Paris for relief work, then made Secretary of Commerce for Harding and Coolidge. He administered flood relief to the Mississippi Valley and rushed food to famine-hit Russia. His hard-driving dynamism, imagination, and efficiency were impressive.

Lou offered hospitality to untold hundreds, actively led the Girl Scout movement, and aided her husband in many ways. She perfected the art of running an elegant household staffed by well-trained servants, a skill very useful in her White House years.

THE GREAT DEPRESSION

The apparently unending prosperity of the Republican regime helped push Hoover into the presidency. Hoover publicly declared his vision of the imminent end of poverty in the United States—little guessing that seven months after his 1929 inauguration the stock market would crash and the Depression would spread like a fungus across America and the world. Hordes of homeless huddled in shanty towns called Hoovervilles, and empty pockets turned inside out were dubbed "Hoover flags." Banks failed, and by 1932, twelve million were unemployed.

Hoover believed passionately in the merits of hard work and somehow imagined that the destitute could pull themselves up by their bootstraps rather than depend on government work programs. He stopped every attempt to organize federal relief and refused to meet with unemployed veterans pleading for assistance. Instead, he sent General Douglas MacArthur and an Army contingent to torch their hovels, injuring scores of men, women and children in the process. Hoover declared, "Thank God we still have a government...that knows how to deal with a mob." Meanwhile, he approved financial aid for industry, and he and Lou continued their White House entertainments, including Blacks and Mormons on their guest lists. Major Executive Mansion remodeling and historic restoration were pet projects.

Badly beaten in the 1932 election, Hoover moved to Stanford, where he occupied himself with the Hoover Institute on War, Revolution, and Peace. In later years, he organized food-distribution for displaced persons in Europe. Presidents Truman and Eisenhower asked him to head commissions to streamline government administration, yielding millions of dollars in savings. Lou died at sixty-nine, but Hoover reached ninety, opinionated and active till the end.

Left: Lou Hoover energetically organized homes in several foreign and American locations and displayed her household skills in the White House, where she arranged cataloging of antique furnishings and historic restoration of several rooms. She lent her talents to designing a rustic Blue Ridge presidential retreat in Virginia and made a point of entertaining minority group guests at the Executive Mansion.

Lou Henry Hoover

Born Mar. 29, 1874, Waterloo, Iowa
Children: 2 sons

Accomplishments:
**Organized complex households in many locations.
President of Girl Scouts of America.
Oversaw historic restoration of key White House rooms.
Designed and had built presidential retreat Camp Rapidan.**

Died age 69, Jan. 7, 1944, New York, N.Y.

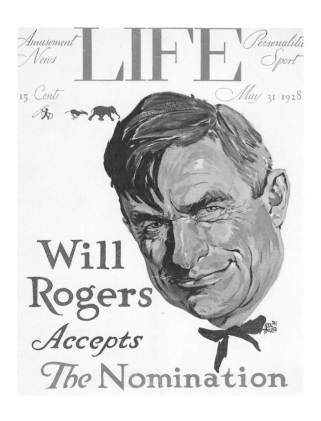

Left: Will Rogers accepts a magazine's presidential "nomination" to bring laughs to the American scene. He mixed homespun humor and social criticism in his popular newspaper columns, lectures, and performances in vaudeville, movies, and on the radio, and the people loved him. Rogers' rope tricks and wry jibes at politicians enlivened the country for three decades, until he died in an Alaska plane crash in 1935.

FRANKLIN DELANO ROOSEVELT

THIRTY-SECOND PRESIDENT
1933-1945
ANNA ELEANOR ROOSEVELT

For more than twelve years, the United States was served by the most brilliant political couple in the nation's history. Franklin Delano Roosevelt—FDR—and his wife Eleanor set precedents for energetic activism that have never been equalled. Guided by commitment to the ideal of helping others, both personally and through the power of government, the Roosevelts devoted their lives to wide-ranging public service. They saw the country through two major trials—the Depression and World War II. For their efforts they earned the love of most of the country's people, but opponents subjected them to constant criticism. Ultimately, it was the public's opinion that mattered—FDR was elected to a record four consecutive presidential terms. The nation came to depend upon Franklin and Eleanor, and when Franklin died in office, the people wept bitterly, as if a close relative had passed away. The sense of loss was lessened by Eleanor's continued moral leadership for another seventeen years.

THE ROOSEVELTS

Franklin and Eleanor were distant cousins, both born into the wealthy Hudson River gentry, traditionally Democratic, imbued with a moral sense that the privileged should help those less fortunate. Theodore Roosevelt, a Republican, was a fifth cousin. They had met briefly at large family gatherings when Franklin was a sheltered but handsome youth under the thumb of his domineering mother and Eleanor was a gawky girl suffering from feelings of inferiority instilled by unthinking relatives who commented on her "ugly duckling" looks.

Eleanor had been orphaned young and dispatched to boarding school in England, where her social conscience was enhanced by her French schoolmistress. Privately educated at home, Franklin imbibed liberal social thought from a Swiss governess. Franklin's mother Sara allowed him to attend Groton and Harvard, where he developed skills in getting along with people of his own age. As the newly swanlike Eleanor was returning from London in 1902, she chanced to meet Franklin and his widowed mother on the train to Hyde Park. The sparks of youthful love caught fire, despite Sara's attempts to stamp them out. In 1905, President Theodore Roosevelt gave the satin-swathed bride away at a St. Patrick's Day wedding in New York City.

Franklin was studying law at Columbia University in New York, so Sara arranged two adjacent houses in East 65th Street—one for the newlyweds and one for her, with connecting doors. Eleanor spent the early years of her marriage raising five children (a sixth died in infancy) and trying to adjust to Sara ruling their lives. At their Hyde Park estate north of the city, Sara remained queen.

Franklin Delano Roosevelt

In Office
Mar. 4, 1933-Apr. 12, 1945
Born Jan. 30, 1882,
Hyde Park, N.Y.
***Party:* Democratic**

Other Offices:
New York State Senator,
1911-13.
Assistant Secretary of the Navy,
1913-20.
New York Governor, 1929-33.

Marriage:
Eleanor Roosevelt Roosevelt,
1905, married 40 yrs.

Presidential Acts (partial):
Declared Bank holiday to
restructure failing banks, 1933.
Initiated the "Hundred Days" of
legislation to produce economic
recovery, including
Civilian Conservation Corps,
Agricultural Adjustment
Administration, Federal
Emergency Relief Act, Tennessee
Valley Authority, Gold Repeal
Joint Resolution, F.D.I.C.,
National Industrial Recovery
Act, and much more, 1933.
Repealed Prohibition, 1933.
Passed Social Security Act, 1935.
Initiated Lend-Lease for Great
Britain, 1941.
Joined with Churchill in The
Atlantic Charter, 1941.
Led the nation through World
War II, 1941-45.

Died age 63,
Apr. 12, 1945,
Warm Springs, Ga.

Left: Franklin Delano Roosevelt became virtually a father figure to millions of Americans. He held office longer than any other chief executive, guiding the nation through the unprecedented crises of Depression and World War II. He grew in stature from a slightly shallow son of privilege to a great statesman seeking justice and peace for the world's peoples.

Left: Seated on the porch at the family estate at Hyde Park, New York in 1906, are Franklin and his bride, Eleanor, a distant cousin. Together they would rear five children, meet the challenge of Franklin's paralysis, and work for the good of the nation. Eleanor once said, "I am in a position where I can do the most good to help the most people."

Anna Eleanor Roosevelt Roosevelt

Born Oct. 11, 1884, New York, N.Y.
Children: **1 daughter, 5 sons**

Accomplishments (partial):
Taught school, edited magazine on babies.
Was deeply involved in her own and her husband's work.
Published columns and books, gave lectures and radio talks.
Responded to hundreds of thousands of letters.
Visited fighting men in Europe, the Pacific, and Latin America.
Delegate to the United Nations, Chairman of Human Rights Commission.
First world stateswoman who was not an official ruler.

Died age 78, Nov. 7, 1962, New York, N.Y.

Right: *Queen Elizabeth of England (now the Queen Mother) and Eleanor Roosevelt ride in an open limousine through the hot streets of Washington in June, 1939, during a goodwill visit of the queen and King George VI, just months before the beginning of World War II. More than half a million cheering people lined the parade route. Friendship between the United States and Britain remained firm throughout the war.*

Franklin and Eleanor grew in independence after his election to the New York Senate, and they established their own home in Albany. A move to Washington followed, when Franklin became Wilson's Assistant Secretary of the Navy. Simple in their tastes, they warmly greeted guests to their home, often with scrambled eggs and cocoa. During the first War, Franklin developed key naval strategies while Eleanor helped out at the Railroad Canteen, serving troops passing through town. In 1919 they traveled together to the Paris Peace Conference, viewing the ruins of war firsthand.

TIMES OF TRIAL

Their marriage was threatened by Eleanor's discovery of love letters revealing an affair between Franklin and Lucy Mercer, Eleanor's lovely secretary. Divorce was averted when Sara threatened to cut her son off without a penny, and Franklin agreed never to see Lucy again. From then on, the marriage was platonic, with the partners free to work together or independently to improve world conditions.

Franklin's robust health and good looks were an asset to the rising politician. In the summer of 1921, at his cottage on Campobello Island on the Maine-Canada border, he came in from a chilling swim—and suffered an attack of polio. He survived, but his legs were paralyzed. Franklin spent the rest of his life struggling with this infirmity, using a wheelchair but learning to stand and walk just enough to create the illusion of good health. He and the press had a gentlemen's agreement not to allow photographs emphasizing his paralysis. He benefited from aquatic therapy at Warm Springs, Georgia, a place he grew to love.

Sara urged Franklin to become an invalid, but with Eleanor's staunch support, Franklin eventually returned to public life. At the same time, Eleanor's role changed dramatically. She became her husband's eyes and ears, moving with increasing confidence into the public arena herself, acting as deputy politician. Coached by newspaperman Louis Howe, Eleanor learned the arts of public relations and speechmaking. The "Franklin-Eleanor team" stepped forward to greatness.

Franklin was twice elected New York's governor and instituted unemployment relief, while Eleanor taught at the Todhunter School in New York and inspected prisons and projects on her husband's behalf. She wrote for magazines and newspapers and spoke on the radio, donating her fees to charity.

THE NEW DEAL

In his 1932 presidential campaign, Roosevelt promised the country a New Deal—equality of opportunity, state benevolence for those in need, and hope for the forgotten man. Hoover was rejected, and FDR won nearly ninety percent of the electoral vote. Against a backdrop of breadlines, increasing millions of unemployed, bank panics, and homeless encampments, Roosevelt was inaugurated, telling the nation, "the only thing we have to fear is fear itself."

FDR's governmental innovations were multitudinous and far-reaching. He moved to solve the banking crisis, cut government salaries and pensions, legalized tax-yielding alcoholic beverages, initiated the giant Tennessee Valley Authority project, and sponsored the National Industrial Recovery Act and the Social Security Act. These measures were followed by many more designed to lift the nation out of the clutches of the Depression and provide security for ordinary citizens. He also reached out to other countries with his "Good Neighbor" policy. Except for his unsuccessful attempt to pack the Supreme Court with extra justices favorable to his plans, he became a world-class master of the art of politics.

Above: *Speaking from the White House on March 12, 1933, in the depths of the Depression, President Roosevelt held his first "fireside chat," broadcasting his comments nationwide. Millions listened to his radio speeches, effective presentations of his policies and plans for the nation's recovery. Author John Gunther remarked that one felt as if he were in the room, speaking to every listener personally.*

The White House rang with gaiety, and Eleanor was often at hand, graciously organizing and overseeing, but she was often away as well, endlessly appearing at slums, union gatherings, mines, and soup kitchens. Her column, "My Day," appeared in newspapers across the country, bringing to the people a sense of intimacy with their leaders.

THE SECOND WORLD WAR

Like Woodrow Wilson, whom he admired, Roosevelt tried to keep the United States out of war. Hitler was on the march in Europe, grabbing territory and instituting the German reign of terror. FDR sent aid to Britain but maintained official neutrality. He won reelection to a third term on the promise that no American boys would be sent to fight in a foreign war. This hope ended on the morning of December 7, 1941, when the Japanese attacked Pearl Harbor. At Roosevelt's passionate urging, Congress declared war on Japan, and shortly thereafter, Germany and Italy.

More than sixteen million Americans served in World War II, and more than 405,000 lost their lives. Worldwide, an estimated 55 million died in the conflict, perhaps the greatest battle between evil and decency the world will ever see. With his radio "fireside chats" and magnetic leadership, FDR inspired the nation to get through years of horrendous crisis. Roosevelt's brilliant personal diplomacy was crucial to the proceedings of three major wartime conferences, at

Casablanca, Teheran, and Yalta. He spoke out for the creation of the United Nations, while Eleanor visited troops all over the world.

Weakened by his illnesses and the strains of war, FDR went to Warm Springs to rest and meet and chat with an old friend, Lucy Mercer. Suddenly, on April 12, 1945, while posing for a portrait, he suffered a massive cerebral hemorrhage and died.

Eleanor rushed south, where she suffered not only the pain of her husband's death but of learning that Lucy had been with FDR at his fatal attack. Grieving, she accompanied her husband's body on the funeral train as it moved past weeping people all along its route. As the war raged toward its conclusion in Europe and Asia, Roosevelt was buried at his beloved childhood home, Hyde Park, on the Hudson River.

Eleanor took a short respite but soon returned to public endeavor. Presidents Truman and Kennedy asked for her help at the United Nations, where she chaired the Human Rights Commission. She became America's conscience, speaking out for social and economic equity in a variety of forums, securing her place as America's greatest First Lady. As Adlai Stevenson said of her, "She would rather light candles than curse the darkness, and her glow has warmed the world." She now lies beside Franklin at Hyde Park.

Above: Showing the effects of illness and stress, FDR sits between Winston Churchill and Joseph Stalin at the Yalta Conference in the Crimea in February, 1945. Churchill could not bear to sit next to Stalin. Standing behind the "Big Three" are Anthony Eden, Edward Stettinius, Vyacheslav Molotov, and W. Averell Harriman. Of the various accords reached at Yalta, the more lasting one was agreement to establish the United Nations.

Right: Roosevelt's body is carried in his funeral procession in Washington, D.C., April 14, 1945. An honor guard and grieving spectators line the route. On hearing the news of his death, people all over the world burst into tears, feeling a desperate sense of loss. Churchill said he felt as if he had been "struck a physical blow." With the war not yet over, the nation groped for new leadership.

Right: Flames and smoke billow from the battleship U.S.S. Arizona on the morning of December 7, 1941, "a day that will live in infamy." On that quiet Sunday morning, some 360 Japanese planes attacked the U.S. Pacific fleet at Pearl Harbor, Hawaii, enraging the nation and bringing America into the war.

HARRY S. TRUMAN

THIRTY-THIRD PRESIDENT
1945-1953
BESS WALLACE TRUMAN

When Eleanor Roosevelt heard the news of her husband's demise, she called Vice President Harry Truman to the White House. She put her arm around him and said, "Harry, the President is dead." Shocked, he asked if he could do anything for her. "Is there anything *we* can do for *you*?" she responded. "For you are the one in trouble now."

For more than twelve years, "the President" meant only one person, the larger-than-life FDR, whose wife was an international activist of renown. Now the title fell to a former men's clothing salesman from a small Missouri town, whose spouse abhorred the public eye. In fact, Bess Truman had hated the idea of her husband becoming vice president, as she realized it could mean he might one day face the awesome responsibilities of president. Her fears were well justified. Yet, remarkably, the job evoked the best in Truman, and he dealt strongly with several major crises at home and abroad. He meant what the sign on his desk said, "The buck stops here." The public grew to like him so much, after he completed FDR's term, against all predictions, he was elected in his own right.

A SMALL-TOWN COUPLE

Harry Truman was born on a Missouri farm, the oldest of three children, and grew up in the small town of Independence, outside Kansas City, Mo. He worked as a bank clerk and railway timekeeper, managed his mother's family farm for some years, and then joined the ranks of artillerymen going off to fight in World War I.

Before leaving for France, Truman was informally engaged to Bess Wallace, a young woman from "the right side of the tracks" in Independence. Bess and Harry had met in grade school; he was enticed by her blonde curls but could never keep up with her athletic abilities. She rode, skated, danced, and played tennis, while bespectacled Harry played the piano but stayed clear of more physical antics. Her father suffered business problems and committed suicide, and her mother became totally dependent on her. Starchy Mrs. Wallace disapproved of a dirt farmer for a son-in-law, but when Harry came back from war as a Major, she was forced to accept him. By then, the couple were in their mid-thirties. Bess wore a short summer frock for her wedding, and the couple honeymooned in Port Huron, Michigan. Their daughter Margaret was born five years later.

Left: Harry Truman, an ordinary man from a small Midwestern town, surprised the country with his ability to come to grips with problems of historic proportions. With firm authority, he faced the challenges of the atomic bomb, the Berlin Blockade, the Cold War, the Korean War, rebuilding Europe, and restructuring the American economy. Later Truman recalled, "I did my damnedest, and that's all there was to it!"

Left: Truman links hands with Churchill and Stalin at Potsdam, Germany, in July, 1945. The new Big Three met to establish territorial lines in Europe and secure Soviet assistance against Japan. Secretly, Churchill held Truman in low regard but later praised him as the man who "saved Western civilization." Distrust between Stalin and the others was mutual. Stalin reneged on previous promises and tightened his grip on the non-Soviet countries of Eastern Europe.

Harry S. Truman

In Office
Apr. 12, 1945-Jan. 20, 1953
Born May 10, 1884, Lamar, Mo.
Party: **Democratic**

Other Offices:
Major, Field Artillery, World War I.
Judge, Jackson Co., Mo., 1922-24, 26-34.
U.S. Senator, 1935-45.
Chairman, Special Senate Committee to Investigate the National Defense Program, 1941-44.
Vice President, 1945.

Marriage:
Elizabeth Wallace Truman, 1919, married 53 yrs.

Presidential Acts:
Authorized signing United Nations Charter, 1945.
Attended Potsdam Conference, 1945.
Authorized detonation of two atomic bombs in Japan, 1945.
Signed Big Four Treaty, 1947.
Initiated Truman Doctrine to combat communism, 1947.
Integrated military services under Secretary of Defense, 1947.
Dealt with Berlin Blockade, 1948.
Pushed for Nuremberg Trials to punish war criminals.
Initiated Marshall Plan, 1948.
Dealt with striking steel, railroad, & mine workers, 1949-52.
Helped organize NATO, 1949.
Acted as Commander-in-Chief during Korean War, 1950-53.

Died age 88,
Dec. 26, 1972,
Independence, Mo.

Below: Bess Truman, at left, stands behind daughter Margaret at a 1948 Midwest campaign gathering. Truman, the most powerful man in the world during his presidency, called his wife "the Boss" and sought her sensible counsel on every issue. She occasionally drank and smoked and once sheepishly asked a White House staff member to replace two slats on Harry's bed since they had broken during the night.

Truman and a partner opened a haberdashery store, but the business failed. With the help of a local Democratic boss, Truman started up the political ladder—first spending years as county "judge"—an administrative post—and then going to the U.S. Senate.

Small-town folks transplanted to the national capital, the Trumans blended in without difficulty. Truman gained prominence by heading a Senate committee investigating inefficient war contracts, bringing his thriftiness and common sense to bear, saving the nation some fifteen billion dollars. For Roosevelt's last campaign, Truman was an offhand choice for the vice-presidential spot, accepting it against Bess's wishes.

THE NUCLEAR AGE BEGINS

Suddenly, the Trumans were in the White House, and the new president was faced with historic issues of major proportions. Before Roosevelt died, Truman had not even known of the existence of the atomic bomb, and now he had to decide whether or not to use it to end the war with Japan. He reluctantly authorized the bombing of Hiroshima and Nagasaki, in which some 150,000 died, and Japan surrendered, thus saving the lives of countless Americans and Japanese who would have perished in an invasion of Japan.

Stalin's intransigience became evident, and the Cold War began. The American armed forces had to be demobilized and integrated into a peacetime economy, industry converted, Germany and Japan occupied and rebuilt, and order restored to war-torn Europe. Truman found himself the leader of what was called the free world, resisting the spread of Soviet conquest and of communism. He enunciated the Truman Doctrine, declaring U.S. support for free peoples resisting subjugation by armed minorities or outsiders.

Truman gave the go-ahead for Secretary of State George Marshall's costly but successful plan to rebuild Europe's economy. He effectively met the threat posed by the Soviet Union's blockade of Berlin and began negotiations for setting up the North Atlantic Treaty Organization (NATO), an alliance of Western nations pledged to mutual support.

Bess firmly resisted all attempts to drag her into the spotlight, preferring instead to be as different from Eleanor Roosevelt as possible. A stout woman, she was always dressed in a ladylike fashion, usually wearing a hat and white gloves in public. The press was so desperate for something to report about her that they wrote about her entertaining the Independence Bridge Club for a weekend in 1946. Actually, Bess had a witty streak and once said she had worked hard to get her husband to use the word "manure" in public rather than a more earthy alternative.

Truman tried to have a Civil Rights bill passed, but enraged southerners made it impossible. Bess and Harry grew beyond their early religious and racial prejudices. When Harry publicly shook a black Texan's hand and the crowd booed, Bess said, "Don't mind them Harry! You did the right thing!"

TRUMAN WINS

Truman confounded his critics during his election campaign by making a highly popular 22,000-mile whistle-stop tour. All predicted that his opponent, Thomas Dewey, would win—but

Elizabeth (Bess) Virginia Wallace Truman

Born Feb. 13, 1885, Independence, Mo.
Children: **1 daughter**

Accomplishments:
**Organized home life, provided valued advice to husband.
Lobbied for White House restoration.
Advocated Food Conservation Austerities.
Died age 97, Oct. 18, 1982, Independence, Mo.**

it was Truman who took the oath of office in January, 1949.

His second term was tormented by the noxious activities of Senator Joseph McCarthy, who, with his henchmen, accused virtually everyone in the country of being a communist and enemy of America. Setting the scene for McCarthy's wild denunciations were the communist revolution in China and the invasion of South Korea. Truman sent Americans into battle on the frigid Korean peninsula, and when General Douglas MacArthur over-

Left: "Dewey Defeats Truman," proclaims the headline in the Chicago Daily Tribune, triumphantly displayed by newly-elected Truman at the St. Louis train station on November 4, 1948. Truman knew how to charm the crowds with his down-home manner. His administration was noted as the most liberal in history. Historian Arnold Tynbee credited him with supporting the most significant achievement of the modern era—the attention lavished on the world's poorer countries by the more privileged nations.

stepped his authority, Truman fired him. MacArthur was hailed as a hero, but Truman had done what he felt he needed to do. In later years, Joseph McCarthy was finally unmasked as the petty destroyer of lives that he was and faded into obscurity and death.

For most of the second term, the Trumans lived in Blair House, across the street from the Executive Mansion, which underwent extensive reconstruction. The house had become structurally unsound. Bess successfully lobbied for historic reconstruction rather than complete replacement. Staying at the smaller Blair House relieved Bess of the need to put on large galas, a task she did not relish. The Trumans were able to enjoy the restored mansion for a short time before the end of Harry's term.

The Trumans retired to Missouri, where the former president worked on his memoirs at the impressive Truman Library, built to preserve the record of his administration. Margaret Truman, who had attempted a singing career, married prominent journalist Clifton Daniel, had four sons, and gained some note as a writer of memoirs and mystery stories.

Left: It fell to Truman to decide to use nuclear weapons for the first time. Two atomic bombs were dropped over Japan, on the cities of Hiroshima and Nagasaki in August 1945, bringing an immediate end to the war. Shown here is one of many atomic tests that began on Bikini atoll in 1946 and continued as the arms race with the Soviet Union developed.

DWIGHT D. EISENHOWER

THIRTY-FOURTH PRESIDENT
1953-1961

MAMIE DOUD EISENHOWER

"I like Ike," was the theme of Dwight Eisenhower's presidential campaign—and of his life. A man of great charm, he used his way with people to the finest advantage in the personal, military, and political spheres. He led the Allied forces to victory over the Axis in World War II and then led his country through a period of relatively prosperous peace. For those who opposed his policies, his bright smile made acceptance easier. He claimed to dislike the social engineering of the Roosevelt and Truman administrations, but important new social reforms occurred under his aegis.

Backing him throughout his adult life was his wife Mamie, a lively mate who loved the color pink, symbol perhaps of the eternal youth she wished could be hers. Her vivacity and devotion to her husband undoubtedly helped his career and prolonged his life.

Eisenhower was one of six sons of a poor Kansas family of a Mennonite sect. His father was a mechanic, his mother a strong-minded religious homemaker, all of whose sons became very successful. Ike found his route to success through the military—first West Point, where he was an average student, and later as a member of General MacArthur's staff.

In 1915, while stationed at Fort Sam Houston near San Antonio, Ike was invited to a friend's house, where he met young Mamie Doud, a sweet-tempered and popular girl. Her family was much more cosmopolitan than Ike's; they lived in Denver but owned a winter home in San Antonio. Ike was persistent in his courtship, and their engagement was soon announced. The bride wore chantilly lace, with a pink sash, and the groom wore dress whites. The young couple set up housekeeping—not once, but twenty-seven times in their years together, moving from place to place on various military assignments, including tropical Panama and the Philippines. Their first child, nicknamed Icky, fell victim to scarlet fever at age three. Their second son, John, survived.

SUPREME COMMANDER

On maneuvers in Louisiana, Ike showed brilliance in planning military tactics, and he came to the notice of General George Marshall, who promoted him over the heads of several others to operational commander in Europe. Ike had spent World War I stateside, but during World

---

Dwight David Eisenhower

In Office
Jan. 20, 1953-Jan. 20, 1961
Born Oct. 1890, Denison, Tex.
Party: **Republican**

Other Offices:
**Major, U.S. Army, 1920-42.
Commanding General, European Theatre of Operations, Commander-in-Chief of Allied forces in North Africa,
Commander of U.S. Occupation forces in Europe, 1942-45.
Chief of Staff, U.S. Army, 1945-48.
President, Columbia University, 1948-50.
Commander of NATO forces in Europe, 1950-52.**

Marriage:
Mamie Doud Eisenhower, 1916, married 52 yrs.

Presidential Acts:
**Ended Korean War, 1953.
Created Dept. of Health, Education & Welfare, 1953.
Authorized & inaugurated St. Lawrence Seaway, 1954-59.
Helped create Southeast Asia Treaty Organization, 1954.
Dealt with Suez Crisis, 1956.
Promulgated Eisenhower Doctrine aiding Middle East countries, 1957.
Sent troops to Little Rock to support school integration, 1957.
Supported Civil Rights Commission, 1957.
Authorized NASA, 1958.
First president licensed to fly an airplane.**

**Died age 78,
Mar. 28, 1969,
Washington, D.C.**

War II, he was Commanding General in the European Theatre, directing the Allied armies in all their campaigns in Africa, Sicily, Italy, France, and Germany. He combined tactical genius with the nerve to make decisions—such as to launch the D-Day landing at Normandy that changed the course of the war and of world history.

Ike's buoyant optimism drew people to him, and many of those he worked with during the war came to idolize him. His photograph was in every newspaper and magazine, and the world adored the image of the boyish-faced general charged with destroying Nazism and restoring moral order to the globe.

For Mamie, however, the war was a time of distressing separations, fears for her husband's life, reading of his purported relationship with his woman driver, and coping with heart disease as well as Meniere's disease, which affected her balance and gave rise to rumor of an alcohol problem. Their marriage was tried, but survived and later flourished.

After the war, the popular Eisenhower was courted by both Democrats and Republicans as a presidential candidate, but he declined all offers. His fame increased with the publication of his war memoirs, *Crusade in Europe*. After serving as president of Columbia University for two years, he returned to Europe to spearhead the creation of military forces for NATO. Finally, in 1952, Ike agreed to head the Republican ticket, with Richard Nixon as his running mate and the witty and intellectual Adlai Stevenson, as his opponent.

AMERICA'S FATHER FIGURE

Mamie loved the fun and fame of the campaign trail and enjoyed bringing pink into the White House decorating scheme. She was not particularly active

Above: *Dressed for a 1954 formal reception at the Ethiopian Embassy, the Eisenhowers pose at the White House. Together for eight years in the Executive Mansion, the couple strengthened their marriage. Just after he took the oath of office, the president kissed his wife—the first such open expression of affection between a presidential couple. Every Valentine's Day, he amused her by wearing his "lovebug" undershorts.*

Above: *Supreme Allied Commander Eisenhower spoke with painted-faced paratroopers of the 101st Airborne Division at Newbury, England, shortly before they dropped into France behind the German lines on D-Day, June 6, 1944. Eisenhower told his forces, "You are about to embark on a great crusade." The highly complex and risky attack turned the tide of the war, the most costly in human history.*

as First Lady, but she devoted much time to answering letters and requests. She focused extensively on clothes, and her trade-mark coiffure with bangs was widely emulated. She tried never to miss her favorite television serial, *As the World Turns*, played a lot of canasta, entertained the stars of *I Love Lucy* as well as numerous heads of state, and spoke out for a few good causes. She and Ike were openly affectionate.

The Eisenhower administration was not a time of stirring leadership, although Ike provided a sense of fatherly comfort to a country entering the fast-paced postwar era. Containing communism at home and abroad remained the key issue. McCarthy continued to hold hearings, until he was finally condemned by the Senate in 1954. The Korean War ended without a true resolution. Taiwan and mainland China threatened each other, and Secretary of State John Foster Dulles played with "brinkmanship," almost provoking the U.S. and the U.S.S.R. to mutual nuclear annihilation. Fidel Castro took over in Cuba and Americans offered only verbal encouragement to the Hungarians, who futilely fought Soviet tanks and troops in the streets of Budapest.

In 1954, the Supreme Court decided that racial segregation in public schools must end, but Ike did little to enforce this until 1957, when he called out federal troops to control rioting in Little Rock. Ike did, however, authorize a Civil Rights Commission, and created the Department of Health, Education, & Welfare. The Soviet Union launched two small space satellites or Sputniks—and the U.S. rushed to establish the National Aeronautics and Space Administration (NASA).

Ike had suffered a heart attack, ileitis, and a slight stroke, each time tenderly restored to health by Mamie's attentions and good medical care. As he finally turned toward retirement, the old war hero warned the nation against the unwarranted influence of the "conjunction of an immense military establishment and a large arms industry" which he believed to have a new and disastrous potential. The Eisenhowers retired to their farm in Gettysburg, Pennsylvania—the first home they had ever owned. Ike enjoyed playing golf and painting, and with his wife, son, daughter-in-law and grandchildren at his side, delighted in eight years of a peaceful life which he had personally fought to preserve for all people of the world.

Left: Mamie Eisenhower took pride in her appearance, wearing fashions appropriate to the fifties. The President once publicly introduced her as "my invaluable, my indispensable, but publicly inarticulate lifelong partner." Mamie chose a low-profile public role but consciously tried to do good, actively and symbolically. She encouraged integration at the White House, held a special reception for the National Council of Negro Women, and asked Mahalia Jackson to sing at her birthday party.

Mamie Geneva Doud Eisenhower

Born Nov. 14, 1896, Boone, Iowa
Children: **2 sons (1 died young)**

Accomplishments:
Helped found women's & children's hospital in Panama. Supported various worthy causes, entertained official guests.

Died age 82, Nov. 1, 1979, Washington, D.C.

Left: Stopping to laugh between shots at Quantico, Virginia, Ike shows the pleasure he took in playing golf. Mamie encouraged her husband to relax, hoping to avoid health problems. After Ike's heart attack, Mamie increased her involvement in fund-raising projects for the American Heart Association, stimulating public support for the organization.

JOHN F. KENNEDY

THIRTY-FIFTH PRESIDENT
1961-1963
JACQUELINE BOUVIER KENNEDY

John F. Kennedy stood bareheaded in the autumn sun on the steps of the University of Michigan Student Union, delivering a 1960 campaign speech. Looking more like a college student than a potential president, he presented the idea of a Peace Corps, sending idealistic young Americans to developing countries, where their expertise might be of use to people seeking to better their lives. The idea was derived from suggestions made earlier by Senators Hubert Humphrey and Richard Neuberger, but something about Kennedy's style made it sound better to the young crowd. It was JFK's charisma, in combination with his intellect and accomplishments, that helped him capture the imagination of the American people.

His presidency would last a bare thousand days, but in that time, he created a legend and a memory that remain strong around the world. Even those too young to remember the man know him from constantly-seen photographs and films and the lingering controversy over his death. An essential part of the memory is his lovely wife Jackie and two tiny children, born to privilege yet suddenly left fatherless by the evil of assassination.

PREPARING FOR THE PRESIDENCY

JFK was the second of nine children of an extremely prosperous Irish Catholic family of Massachusetts. His multimillionaire father, Joseph P. Kennedy, built a fortune through questionable means during Prohibition and became Ambassador to Great Britain. His mother, Rose Fitzgerald Kennedy, daughter of a former mayor of Boston, was the glue that held the family together. The clan spent much time at their compound at Hyannisport, on Cape Cod. JFK's older brother, Joseph Jr., was primed to seek the presidency, but when he died in the war, the family's focus fell on Jack, as he was known. Jack cheerfully took up the challenge, with his family's extensive moral and financial support.

After graduating from Harvard, Jack joined the Navy and requested sea duty. For his efforts as commander of a Navy patrol boat in saving the lives of his men, he received a medal for heroism, and his account of the episode, *PT-109*, became a popular book and motion picture.

Kennedy ran for Congress and won, with the help of his entire clan and all their friends. He went on to serve three terms before defeating Henry Cabot Lodge for a Senate seat and was known as the most eligible bachelor in the Senate—but not for long.

Jacqueline Bouvier had grown up in privileged settings in the New York and Washington areas. Poised and beautiful, she was pronounced Debutante of the Year by a newspaper colum-

Left: President John F. Kennedy and his little son John Jr. ("John-John"), walk hand in hand at the White House. Kennedy and his young family brought a vigorous new spirit to the Executive Mansion. Only forty-three at his inauguration, Kennedy was the youngest man elected to the presidency. In his thousand days in office, JFK gave the nation a sense of promise and purpose.

Left: President Kennedy meets in the Oval Office with Secretary of State Dean Rusk and Secretary of Defense Robert McNamara during the Cuban Missile Crisis. The most serious challenge to Kennedy's leadership, the crisis might have led to war. Kennedy demanded that Soviet Premier Nikita Khrushchev remove the offensive missiles he had installed in 1962 Cuba, pointing to the U.S. just ninety miles away—and Khrushchev did so.

nist. She attended Vassar and studied in Paris, polishing her French. She joined the journalistic world as "The Inquiring Camera Girl," interviewing Washington notables—including handsome Senator Kennedy. Their society wedding at Newport was a great gala, with 1,700 guests gathered on a lawn overlooking Narragansett Bay.

The fairytale lifestyle was lovely yet disturbed by difficulties. Jackie adjusted to the busy life demanded of a Kennedy family member and a politician's wife. Jack underwent serious spinal surgery, almost dying, and Jackie lost two babies through miscarriage and stillbirth. Finally, Caroline was born in 1957, and John Jr. in 1960. Another son, Patrick, died shortly after birth in 1963. Jack's book, *Profiles in Courage,* written while he was convalescing, won a Pulitzer Prize. Later, reports of womanizing and a special friendship with Marilyn Monroe would surface, but these were not made public during Kennedy's lifetime.

Jack's opponent in the 1960 election was Richard Nixon, Eisenhower's Vice President. The two met in four televised debates, and charming JFK made an impressive appearance. He went on to win the election, though by only a tiny margin of popular votes.

THE THOUSAND DAYS OF CAMELOT

JFK's eloquent inaugural address set the tone for his administration: "Ask not what your country can do for you—ask what you can do for your country." Kennedy set his "New Frontier" in motion, unveiling many new major domestic programs. Food for Peace was expanded, the Peace Corps became reality, and the Alliance for Progress for Latin American cooperation began.

Above: *Jacqueline Kennedy personified elite dignity in her position as First Lady. Idolized around the world for her beauty and taste in fashions, she gracefully combined privacy and public diplomacy. This portrait by Aaron Shikler hangs in the White House, which she imbued with a touch of cultured charm. Jackie's idea for a National Cultural Center blossomed into the reality of the John F. Kennedy Center for the Performing Arts.*

A spirit of vivacity and culture permeated the White House. Elegance of manner and mind characterized the gatherings organized by the youngest man ever elected to the presidency and the most beautiful First Lady of modern times. Jackie, who considered her children her first priority, oversaw a major historic redecoration of the White House interior. Nobel Prize winners came to dinner, Robert Frost read poems, and Pablo Casals played his cello. John Kenneth Galbraith, distinguished professor and ambassador, traded literary tips with the new president. Some described the new administration as an almost magical "Camelot."

Kennedy faced both domestic and international crises of great significance. He supported an attempt by Cuban dissidents to invade Cuba at the Bay of Pigs, but this failed miserably. A crisis in Laos was averted, and the presidential couple traveled to Berlin to remind Nikita Khrushchev of American interests there. In Paris, Jackie charmed De Gaulle with her beauty and fluency in French. Later, Jackie made a goodwill tour of India. The Soviets brought missiles and men to Cuba, and Kennedy faced the Soviets down, forcing withdrawal and narrowly averting war.

Civil rights were hotly contested, especially in Mississippi and Alabama, where federal troops were sent to insure that black students could attend integrated classes. More than 200,000 civil rights marchers demonstrated in Washington, and Kennedy introduced major civil rights legislation. The president of South Vietnam was assassinated, and Americans took tentative steps into that quagmire.

TRAGEDY IN DALLAS

Younger and fresher than any previous administration, the Kennedy White House seemed pointed toward beneficial social and economic changes coupled with intellectual and cultural accomplishment. But the promise was to remain unfulfilled. The Kennedys traveled to Dallas, where they rode in an open car in a motorcade. Shots rang out, and the President slumped in his seat, mortally wounded. Spattered with blood, Jackie cradled her dying husband and saw him breathe his last.

Vice President Johnson was hastily sworn in on the plane bearing the president's body back to Washington, Jackie in her stained pink suit at his side. Through four days of official mourning and a state funeral, the stunned nation wept. The sight of the young widow, veiled in black and holding the hands of her two innocent children, was widely broadcast on television, tugging at the heartstrings of the world.

Several years later, Jackie married Greek shipping magnate Aristotle Onassis. After his death, she worked in New York as a book editor and maintained a strictly private life. In the spring of 1994, she succumbed to cancer, meeting death with as much dignity as she had lived life.

> ### Jacqueline Lee Bouvier Kennedy
>
> **Born July 28, 1929, Southampton, N.Y.**
> ***Children:* 1 daughter, 2 sons (1 son died in infancy)**
>
> ***Accomplishments:***
> **Aided in entertaining and diplomacy.**
> **Directed historic restoration of White House interior, established White House Historical Association.**
>
> **Died age 64, May 19, 1994, New York, N.Y.**

Left: Jackie Kennedy personally directed a historical restoration of the White House interior, bringing together American and European antiques with period wallcoverings, hangings, and arrangements. The White House became an elegant yet functional background for the presidency, complete with historical pieces, such as this Lincoln portrait hanging in the State Dining Room. The Kennedy program was institutionalized in the White House Historical Association, permanent caretaker of the presidential home.

Above: As sorrow engulfed the nation, the flag-draped casket of the slain president was taken to the East Room for twenty-four hours, where those close to him could kneel in silence. It was then moved to the Capitol Rotunda to lie in state. Hundreds of thousands of mourners filed past the guarded coffin, and representatives of over ninety countries attended the state funeral.

Right: Lyndon B. Johnson was a brilliant politician who knew his way around the halls of the Capitol perhaps better than any president in recent history. Following a president noted as a cultured intellectual, the more earthy Johnson sometimes defended himself by saying, "They say Jack Kennedy had style, but I'm the one who got the bills passed." Johnson's legislative successes were unparalleled.

Lyndon Baines Johnson

In Office
Nov. 22, 1963-Jan. 20, 1969
Born Aug. 27, 1908,
near Stonewall, Tex.
Party: Democratic

Other Offices:
U. S. Congressman, 1937-49.
Lt. Commander, U.S.Navy,
1941.
Commander, U.S. Naval
Reserve, 1948.
U.S. Senator, 1949-61.
Vice President, 1961-63.

Marriage:
Lady Bird Taylor Johnson, 1934,
married 39 yrs.

Presidential Acts:
Enacted "Great Society" laws,
including aid to Appalachia,
Medicare, Voting Rights Law,
housing program, anti-poverty
program, educational aid,
increase in minimum wage,
1965-66.
Created Dept. of Housing &
Urban Development, 1965.
Enacted legislation for auto and
highway safety, 1966.
Dealt with problems in Panama,
Dominican Republic, 1964-65.
Directed American involvement
in Vietnam War, 1963-69.
Met Soviet Premier Kosygin at
Glassboro, N.J. Summit, 1967.
Appointed first black,
Thurgood Marshall, to
Supreme Court, 1967.
Initiated Vietnam Peace Talks,
1968.

Died age 64, Jan. 22, 1973,
San Antonio, Tex.

LYNDON B. JOHNSON

THIRTY-SIXTH PRESIDENT
1963-1969
LADY BIRD JOHNSON

Lyndon Johnson was one of America's most consummate politicians. He knew how to direct the players in the game of politics the way a great conductor knows how to direct musicians in playing a symphony. Johnson's energy has been compared to that of a speeding train, rushing ahead and letting nothing stand in the way of reaching his goals. Unconstrained by the polite etiquette of the East, he practiced a Texan earthiness that anyone could understand. He knew the needs of the common people and successfully shaped his domestic programs to fit those needs.

Unfortunately, he stumbled badly in foreign affairs; the Vietnam War finished his political career.

Johnson came to the presidency in a moment of national grief—the body of his murdered predecessor was only a few feet away on the presidential plane when he took the oath of office. Johnson had come to that place not by surprise but through years of ambitious striving.

THE TEXAS FARMBOY

Descended from early Texas settlers and a former governor of Kentucky, Johnson was a brash youth used to farm work in the hard soil of the hill country of southwestern Texas. He worked at various jobs, including laboring on a road gang. Finally, his college-educated mother coaxed him into going to college. He breezed through in three years, did some teaching, and got involved in politics. From then on, the only direction he went was up. He was secretary to a Texas congressman, administrator of FDR's National Youth Administration in Texas, and then became a young congressman himself. FDR took him under his wing, and in 1941, Johnson tried for the Senate—and lost. He volunteered for active naval duty in the War and was in a plane shot down by the Japanese over New Guinea. For showing "marked coolness," he was awarded the Silver Star Medal.

Awaiting his return from the battle zone was his dynamic wife, Claudia, known as Lady Bird. Daughter of a wealthy east Texas family, she had been raised by her father, an aunt, and servants, after her mother was fatally knocked down a flight of steps by a dog when Lady Bird was a child of six. She graduated from the University of Texas at Austin, where she majored in journalism because "people in the press...had more exciting things happen to them." Excitement entered her life suddenly when she chanced to meet Lyndon in a friend's office, and he fell in love with her at first sight. He swooped her up in his net of persuasive charm, and they rushed into marriage. She proved an ideal mate for a political whirlwind.

Lady Bird ran LBJ's congressional office for him while he was on active duty, and she shrewdly invested an inheritance in an Austin television station. The station would make the Johnsons among the wealthiest inhabitants of the White House. They bought ranches and made their favorite, the LBJ, into a showplace. Lady Bird suffered a series of miscarriages but finally gave birth to two daughters, Lynda Bird and Luci Baines. LBJ ran for the Senate in 1948 and won the Democratic primary by just eighty-seven votes. Whether those votes were legally obtained has been a subject of dispute, but it was through this victory that LBJ clinched his spot in the higher echelons of Washington power. Lady Bird was an active campaigner in that election and others to follow. Barbecues and appearances by the little girls became part of LBJ's effective campaign machinery.

By 1954, Johnson was Senate majority leader, using his personal skills to manipulate other legislators to do his bidding. He was disappointed to lose the presidential nomination to Kennedy but accepted the vice-presidential spot. The ticket won narrowly—that it won at all was at least partly due to LBJ's way with southern voters and to Lady Bird's engaging campaign activities—including great cordiality to black voters.

THE GREAT SOCIETY

The events in Dallas behind him, Johnson picked up the torch of humanitarian government that had been handed down to him by FDR, Truman, and JFK. Johnson urged Congress to pass the legislation proposed by Kennedy. With relentless persuasiveness, he shepherded through Congress the historic Civil Rights Act of 1964, a huge antipoverty program, including foodstamps, the Job Corps, and aid for mass transit. He defused a railroad labor dispute and ended trouble from Castro over the U.S. base at Guantanamo Bay.

Dogging the dynamic president was the Vietnam issue, which had been slowly snowballing for three previous administrations. Now an avalanche of trouble was thundering his way. In the 1964 reelection campaign, Johnson said he would not escalate the war but would instead concentrate on building "the Great Society...where the meaning of man's life matches the marvel of man's labor." Asian wars were for Asian boys to fight, he maintained. Johnson was elected by the widest margin in history until that time.

Through his phenomenal leadership, Johnson pushed through a blitz of legislation for educational aid, Medicare, Appalachian assistance, fair housing, exploration of space, and the historic Voting Rights Act of 1965.

Below: Lady Bird Johnson deeply adored nature, and even her nickname reflected her spiritual bonds to natural beauty. As a child she delighted in spring magnolias and daffodils, and she later translated her affection for flowers into a national highway beautification project. In her marriage she combined charm with sagacity, and Johnson once said that voters "would happily have elected her over me."

Lady Bird (Claudia) Taylor Johnson

Born Dec. 22, 1912, Karnack, Tex.
Children: 2 daughters

Accomplishments:
Raised family, organized households.
Built family fortune with television station.
Campaigned vigorously for her husband.
Made good will trips to 33 countries.
Active in Head Start, War-on-Poverty Program.
Directed major beautification plan for America.

Above: Johnson used the telephone as a tool in his efforts to get favorite bills passed. He personally phoned legislators to ask for support, disarming them with his dynamic persuasiveness. Johnson loved politics and knew how to cultivate the people in power as well as the voters who put them there.

Lady Bird translated her love of nature into a popular project to beautify America. Removing the blight of billboards from highways was an important ingredient in her plan, which also involved planting wildflowers along roadways. She was a hospitable hostess at numerous White House events, and organized grand weddings for her daughters.

WAR IN VIETNAM

Johnson could not dodge Vietnam. A Viet Cong attack on American troops at Pleiku triggered a spiralling escalation of the war. By the end of 1965, 165,00 Americans were fighting in Vietnam, and bombings, minings, deaths, injuries, strafings, and atrocities were the subjects of daily news broadcasts. Many Americans—the "Doves"—rose in protest against involvement in the war, while others—the "Hawks"—urged military escalation. The nation was divided more than it had been since the Civil War. By 1968, a half-million Americans were fighting in Southeast Asia, and thousands were burning their draft cards back home. In 1968, the war cost was more than $2 billion per month.

Blacks dissatisfied with the conditions of their lives rioted in urban slums, and Martin Luther King, Jr. was shot down in 1968. Democratic Senator Eugene McCarthy entered primaries and won on a platform of total opposition to Vietnam involvement. JFK's brother, Robert Kennedy, attacked Johnson's war policy as "bankrupt," before he too was assassinated. The Viet Cong attacked South Vietnamese cities with unprecedented force, the North Koreans tweaked Uncle Sam's nose by seizing the ship *Pueblo*, and television news showed ever more horrendous scenes of destruction. The Midas of politicians was losing his golden touch, and support fell away.

On March 31, 1968, Johnson dramatically announced that he would not seek his party's nomination in the upcoming election. He suspended bombing and invited North Vietnam to the peace table to begin what would be a long process of negotiation.

Gracefully withdrawing from public life, LBJ returned with Lady Bird to the quiet of his beloved Texas land along the Pedernales River. His trademark Stetson firmly in place, he walked the earth where his forebears had staked their claims, dying there of a heart attack in 1973. Lady Bird took pleasure in her grandchildren and continued her work for beautifying the environment for many years thereafter.

Right: Names of Americans who died in Vietnam make poignant reading at the Vietnam Veterans Memorial built in Washington, D.C. in 1982. One of the most frequently-visited sites in America, the memorial serves as a cathartic reminder of the struggle which rent asunder not only Vietnam but also the United States, where opinions on American involvement were strongly divided.

Right: Police drag a civil rights demonstrator down the steps of the U.S. Capitol, where he was part of a 1965 sit-in. Despite rapid progress in civil rights legislation during the Kennedy and Johnson years, civil rights demonstrations were common. Protesters also expressed bitter opposition to American involvement in the Vietnam war.

RICHARD M. NIXON

THIRTY-SEVENTH PRESIDENT
1969-1974
PATRICIA RYAN NIXON

Richard Nixon's name evokes strong opinions—many remember him as a hard-nosed fighter of corruption and communism who had the foresight to meet the Communist Chinese with an open hand of friendship, while others recall him as a deceiver willing to ignore ethics to retain political power. However history judges him, he is unique as the only president of the United States to resign from office. Standing stalwartly at his side through the ups and downs of his career was his remarkable wife, Pat.

YOUTH AND MARRIAGE

Richard Nixon knew hard work as a child. One of five sons of a Quaker family, Richard was born in a small farm village near Los Angeles. In his youth in the town of Whittier, he worked at the small store that supported the family, and picked crops, did odd jobs, and worked as a teenaged barker at an Arizona rodeo. He watched two youthful brothers die—one of tuberculosis, another of meningitis, because the family could not afford adequate medical care.

Dick Nixon excelled in academics and student politics and graduated from Whittier College with a scholarship for Duke University Law School. He returned to Whittier to practice, and there he met a pretty schoolteacher, Pat Ryan.

Pat had experienced true hardship. Born in a Nevada mining town to a miner father, by seventeen she had lost both parents and set out on her own, working her way through the University of Southern California to graduate with honors. She held many jobs, including bank janitor, store clerk, telephone operator, and bit-player in a movie. When she met Nixon, she was earning $190 a month teaching and coaching cheer leaders at Whittier's high school.

Dick was immediately attracted to Pat, and, after dating her for a while, proposed marriage. Pat told friends that he would be President some day. They were married the next month and set off in a car on a rambling honeymoon. Life promised to be pleasant but ordinary.

Nixon served his World War II naval duty as a supply officer assigned to Pacific base areas, while Pat was employed as an economist in a government office in San Francisco. After Nixon's return, Pat had her first daughter, Tricia, in 1946, and in 1948, a second daughter, Julie.

MOVING INTO POLITICS

Feeling himself an outsider, Nixon worked to join the favored few inside the gates of power. He entered Republican politics and was elected to a congressional seat held by a Democrat whom Nixon accused of being a communist sympathizer. In 1950, Nixon won a Senate seat in a mud-slinging campaign in which he printed a pamphlet about his opponent Helen Douglas, a friend of Eleanor Roosevelt's, on bright pink paper, implying communist leanings. Pat campaigned actively in all Nixon's campaigns, spontaneously mingling with huge crowds.

Richard Milhous Nixon

In Office
Jan. 20, 1969-Aug. 9, 1974
Born Jan. 9, 1913,
Yorba Linda, Calif.
Party: **Republican**

Other Offices:
U.S. Congressman, 1947-51.
U.S. Senator, 1951-53.
Vice President, 1953-61.

Marriage:
Patricia Ryan Nixon, 1940,
married 53 yrs.

Presidential Acts:
Proposed "New Federalism" legislation, including revenue sharing, draft lottery, tax changes, 1969.
Spoke with astronauts on the moon, 1969.
Established Environmental Protection Agency, 1970.
Visited China, 1972.
Completed withdrawal of U.S. forces from Vietnam, 1973.
Ended military draft, 1973.
Became involved in Watergate Scandal, resigned from office, 1974.

Died age 81,
Apr. 22, 1994,
New York, N.Y.

Left: Driven to succeed, Richard M. Nixon rose through education and intelligence from a childhood spent picking beans and pumping gas to the highest political position in America. He ended U.S. combat in Vietnam and opened lines of communication with Communist China that had been closed for decades. But he was unique in being the only U.S. president to resign from office.

Left: President and Mrs. Nixon stand with Chinese leaders at the Great Wall, near Beijing, in February, 1972, thus breaking a long-standing impasse between the U.S. and China. The first president to visit a nation not recognized by the United States, Nixon conferred with Chairman Mao Tse-tung and Premier Chou En-lai. After the historic visit, trade, diplomatic ties, and cultural exchanges expanded dramatically.

Thelma Catherine (Patricia) Ryan Nixon

Born Mar. 16, 1912, Ely, Nev.
Children: 2 daughters.

Accomplishments:
Held numerous jobs, worked her way through college.
Supported educational programs and self-help projects.
Traveled widely on public missions.
Supported her husband throughout times of crisis.

Died age 81, June 22, 1993, Park Ridge, N.J.

Nixon gained fame as a member of the House Un-American Activities Committee, zealously prosecuting Alger Hiss, who was jailed for perjury. When Eisenhower was nominated for president in 1952, his party acclaimed Nixon for the vice-presidential spot.

Nixon's crusade against communism and corruption was interrupted by accusations against his own integrity. He responded to these charges with a famous televised speech, in which he stated that the only political gift he had accepted was a small dog named "Checkers." The speech was convincing enough to save his place on the ticket.

Eisenhower was proud of him and called him, "*my* boy." Throughout Ike's eight-year presidency, Nixon conducted important assignments, attended all key meetings, and was Acting President during Ike's illnesses. In a well-publicized "kitchen debate," Nixon spent five hours talking to Soviet Premier Nikita Khrushchev at an American home display in Moscow.

DEFEAT AND VICTORY

Ike endorsed Nixon to succeed him, but it was not to be. By a close margin, the upstart Kennedy carried the 1962 election. Nixon ran unsuccessfully for California governor, and, intending to leave politics, told the press, "You won't have Dick Nixon to kick around any more."

The Nixons moved from beautiful Beverly Hills to a Fifth Avenue apartment in New York, where Nixon earned more than $200,000 annually at a law firm. With Johnson's descending popularity, Nixon decided to try a political comeback. He cultivated a new smiling image and confidently faced off against liberal Hubert Humphrey in a hotly contested election. At last, as Pat had predicted, Richard Nixon became President of the United States.

Above: *Pat Nixon receives a souvenir feather from Big Bird, a character from television's Sesame Street, at a 1970 children's Christmas party at the White House. Although she presented a serene public facade, Pat felt things deeply and preserved a strong sense of personal balance and compassion. She faithfully stood by her husband in triumph and disgrace.*

Right: *Tricia Nixon married her beau, Edward Finch Cox, in a formal White House wedding in June, 1971. The bride and groom joyously depart through the North Portico doorway of the Executive Mansion. President and Mrs. Nixon stand at right, and the bride's sister Julie, wearing an organza hat, waves from the rear, in the center of the doorway.*

Pledging to seek peace, Nixon focused on ending American involvement in Vietnam. The Paris peace talks proceeded at a snail's pace, while "Vietnamization" of the war dragged out. More protests and demonstrations swept the nation, and National Guardsmen killed four students at Kent State University. Nixon stepped-up the attack on North Vietnam and authorized bombing of Cambodia and Laos.

In a surprise move, Nixon opened relations with Communist China, becoming the first sitting president to visit China. He also visited the Soviet Union and signed nuclear weapons agreements. At home, reforms were effected in tax laws, the voting age, revenue sharing, and payments to the needy. Through a special telephone hookup, Nixon spoke to American astronauts as they walked on the moon for the first time in human history, on July 20, 1969.

Life at the White House was calm. Daughters Tricia and Julie were married, and Pat urged Americans to volunteer for social work and traveled across the country to urge people to make volunteerism the "in" thing to do.

Nixon readily won reelection in 1972 and shortly reached agreement with the other participants in the Vietnam hostilities to end the fighting and exchange prisoners. American forces were pulled out, and the bombing of Cambodia ended.

WATERGATE

The Watergate affair blindsided Nixon's administration. Arising from a burglary of the Democratic Party headquarters in the Watergate building complex in 1972, the scandal broadened to implicate a number of key Nixon employees in the break-in. Nixon firmly declared no knowledge of the original crime or coverup, but his own office tape-recordings, subpoenaed in court, revealed a tissue of lies. Nixon's taped conversations clearly revealed that he knew much more than he had admitted and had ordered a coverup. While the original crime was not huge, the integrity of Nixon and his closest associates was destroyed, and impeachment hearings began. The press gleefully helped uncover misdeeds.

Nixon was charged with obstruction of justice, abuse of presidential powers, and disobeying subpoenas. Congressional leaders told Nixon he would certainly be removed from office unless he resigned. Nixon addressed the nation on television and announced his decision. On August 9, 1974, he submitted his resignation and with his family, flew away to retirement in California. He later moved to the East Coast, wrote his memoirs, and nursed the long-suffering Pat, until her death in 1993. Nixon followed her less than a year later. His funeral was respectfully attended by all five living men who occupied the presidency after he did.

Above: Hurting with the pain of disgrace, former President Nixon bravely signals victory as he prepares to leave the White House grounds on August 9, 1974. Involvement in the Watergate scandal cost him the support of Congress and the nation, and he was forced to resign from office. However, with the passage of time he came to be regarded as an elder statesman.

Right: Having reached the presidency via an unusual route, Gerald R. Ford let sunlight into the White House after a dark and difficult period. His natural good humor and cheerful dedication to teamwork helped restore normalcy to the presidency. A onetime college All-Star football player and graduate of Yale Law School, he encouraged Americans to put the past behind them and work together for the future.

Gerald Rudolph Ford

In Office
Aug. 9, 1974-Jan. 20, 1977
Born July 14, 1913,
Omaha, Neb.
Party: **Republican**

Other Offices:
Lt. Commander, U.S. Navy, 1946.
U.S. Congressman, 1949-73.
Vice President, 1973.

Marriage:
Elizabeth Bloomer Ford, 1948.

Presidential Acts:
Pardoned former President Nixon, 1974.
Conferred with Leonid Brezhnev in Vladivostok on nuclear limitations, 1974.
Initiated investigation of CIA, 1975.
Ordered evacuation of all Americans in Vietnam, 1975.

GERALD R. FORD

THIRTY-EIGHTH PRESIDENT
1974-1977
ELIZABETH BLOOMER FORD

Once voted the most popular high school senior in Grand Rapids, Michigan, Gerald Ford brought an engaging smile and manner to the White House, too long suffused in gloom and ill humor. His wife Betty breathed refreshing candor and a mature attitude toward women's experiences into the role of First Lady.

Ford became vice president and then president without having been elected to either office. When Vice President Spiro Agnew was forced to resign for graft, President Nixon appointed House Minority Leader Ford to fill the gap. When Nixon himself resigned a few months later, Ford was sworn in as President.

Jerry Ford was born in Omaha and originally named Leslie L. King, Jr., after his father, from whom his mother was divorced when he was two. He was later renamed for his mother's second husband, Gerald R. Ford, a paint dealer in Grand Rapids who adopted him. Both his biological parents had children by their other marriages, so Ford had six half-siblings. The parents with whom he grew up were active in volunteer work.

Jerry excelled in sports, got good grades, waited tables, became an Eagle Scout, and worked as a Yellowstone park ranger. At the University of Michigan he played center on the undefeated football team, was voted Most Valuable Player, and was a 1935 college All-American. He went on to coach at Yale and graduated from law school there in the top third of his class. During the War, he was assigned to a ship in the Pacific and was discharged as a lieutenant commander. Ford moved from a law career to Congress, where he remained for thirteen terms, until fate tapped him on the shoulder.

Jerry met beautiful Betty Bloomer in Grand Rapids, where she was teaching dance and working as executive fashion coordinator for a department store. A young divorcee, she had been a fashion model and member of the Martha Graham dance group in New York—she had once performed at Carnegie Hall. Betty had grown up following fashion trends set by First Ladies and was an admirer of Eleanor Roosevelt's independence and willingness to express her own views.

Ford was campaigning on the day of his wedding and arrived late for the ceremony—but their union has persisted for nearly five decades. They have four children.

The public welcomed honest Ford to the presidency but disapproved when he issued a pardon for Nixon for any and all federal crimes he might have committed as President. Ford felt it was time to leave Watergate behind and focus on solving current issues.

The Vietnam War ended for America in April, 1975, with the ignominious departure of the last Americans by helicopter from the roof of the American Embassy in Saigon as the communists took over Vietnam. Ford arranged for some 100,000 refugees to enter the U.S.

Betty Ford had barely set up housekeeping in the Executive Mansion when she was diagnosed with breast cancer and underwent radical surgery. She broke an unspoken taboo and candidly discussed her illness with the public, hoping to encourage other women to seek early diagnosis and treatment. Recovered, she hosted White House functions and campaigned for adoption of the unsuccessful Equal Rights Amendment mandating equal treatment for men and women. In later years, she admitted receiving treatment for alcohol dependency and established the highly acclaimed Betty Ford Center in Rancho Mirage, California, where patients with substance abuse problems are treated. She also openly spoke about her "new look," accomplished with a face lift.

Because he had lost his footing a couple of times, Ford was affectionately lampooned on the television show *Saturday Night Live*, with comedian Chevy Chase making exaggerated pratfalls to parody him.

In seeking election in his own right in 1976, Ford was blamed for the high rates of inflation and unemployment troubling the nation. Candidate Jimmy Carter debated Ford on television and convinced the electorate he could do a better job than Ford in solving the country's problems. The Fords cheerfully retired to a life of leisure and outdoor activity.

Elizabeth (Betty) Bloomer Ford

Born Apr. 8, 1918, Chicago, Ill.
Children: **3 sons, 1 daughter**

Accomplishments:
**Worked as fashion executive, model & dancer, taught dance to handicapped and minority children.
Organized home life, raised 4 children.
Publicized breast cancer awareness.
Supported Equal Rights Amendment.
Founded Betty Ford Center.**

Left: *Betty Ford recovers from her bout with cancer, her husband at her side, reading get-well wishes from Washington friends. In openly discussing her health issues with the public, Betty gained the admiration of millions. She knew the power of the First Lady as a role model for the nation and used her position to further honest assessment of real problems.*

Left: *Homey pleasures are enjoyed on Christmas morning at a gathering in Vail, Colorado, of the Fords, their three sons, daughter, daughter-in-law, and dogs. During the Ford presidency, only one of the Ford children, Susan, resided in the White House. The Fords lived a relaxed life style, impressing visitors with their personal warmth and hospitality. In 1974 they invited over 900 guests to a White House Christmas party. The Fords were especially enthusiastic dancers. They retired to Vail after their years in Washington.*

Right: President Jimmy Carter used his gentle speaking voice to persuade old enemies to come together at various trouble spots around the globe, both during and after his presidency. Carter was an outspoken advocate of human rights, which he expressed in his policy of suspending American aid to nations chronically violating human rights.

James Earl Carter, Jr.

In Office
Jan. 20, 1977-Jan. 20, 1981
Born Oct. 1, 1924, Plains, Ga.
Party: Democratic

Other Offices:
Lt. Commander, U.S. Navy, 1946-53.
Georgia State Senator, 1963-66.
Governor of Georgia, 1971-75.

Marriage:
Rosalynn Smith Carter, 1946.

Presidential Acts:
Pardoned Vietnam War draft resisters, 1977.
Established Depts. of Energy, Education, 1977, 1979.
Expanded national park system.
Signed treaty with Panama, 1978.
Facilitated Camp David Accords between Israel & Egypt, 1978.
Negotiated SALT II Nuclear Limitation Treaty with U.S.S.R., 1979.
Established full diplomatic relations with China, 1979.
Appointed record numbers of women and minorities to government jobs.
Struggled with Iran Hostage Crisis, 1979-81.

JIMMY CARTER

**THIRTY-NINTH PRESIDENT
1977-1981**

ROSALYNN SMITH CARTER

Kindly, soft-spoken Jimmy Carter stood before the crowd on his inauguration day and announced his commitment to improving conditions for all Americans and to enhancing global human rights. Then, he and his wife Rosalynn, holding hands and eschewing their official limousine, walked the mile and a half from the Capitol to the White House, waving to spectators along the way. Their nine-year-old daughter Amy and other members of the family joined them in their walk. Thus, in the first moments of the Carter presidency, the American people glimpsed the essential character of the new President and First Lady—dedication to human values, family affection, and a simple style unaffected by ostentation.

COMMON BACKGROUND

Both Jimmy and Rosalynn were born in Plains, Georgia, a small town set amid fertile farmland. Jimmy grew up, along with two sisters and a brother, helping run the family peanut farm. He was an excellent student and was thrilled to be appointed to the U.S. Naval Academy in Annapolis, Md.

Rosalynn Smith's life in Plains was not easy, especially after her father died when she was thirteen. The eldest of four children, she worked as a cleaning girl in a beauty shop to help pay expenses. When she was just seventeen, Jimmy came home from Annapolis for a visit and took her on a date. Love-struck Jimmy confided to his mother that he wanted to marry Rosalynn. The couple wed when the bride was still eighteen. They would raise four children together.

Carter carried out numerous assignments during his years in the Navy, including engineering officer on a nuclear submarine. Rosalynn enjoyed living in various places as a military wife and was disappointed when Jimmy decided to return home to manage the family businesses after his father died.

Carter worked his way up in state politics, fighting laws discriminating against blacks. As Governor, he declared, "The time for racial discrimination is over." He threw himself into administrative reform and opened many job opportunities for minorities. He decided to seek the presidency, and though little-known when he began, he vigorously campaigned in many state primaries and secured the Democratic nomination on the first ballot.

STRIVING FOR PEACE

Carter promised to deal with the high unemployment and inflation rates that plagued Ford's administration, but despite his best efforts, he was not notably successful. He pardoned Vietnam War draft dodgers, inaugurated new Departments of Energy and Education, and instituted numerous liberal and humanitarian policies. An energy crisis developed, and Carter urged conservation measures.

Carter's most notable achievements were in foreign, rather than domestic, affairs. With sensitive and skillful personal diplomacy, he brought together the leaders of Israel and Egypt, enemies for three decades, to work out a peace agreement. He also signed key treaties with the Soviet Union and Panama.

Rosalynn traveled on a major diplomatic mission to Latin America and dedicated herself to the cause of mental health. She used the power of her position to aid many other causes, notably refugees in Southeast Asia and the Equal Rights Amendment. She preferred modest, informal White House entertainments and eliminated the practice of having trumpeters announce the presidential family.

Despite Carter's accomplishments, a clash with the new fundamentalist rulers of Iran finished his presidency. Looking for scapegoats, the followers of the Ayatollah Khomeini seized the U.S. Embassy in Teheran and held sixty-six Americans hostage for fourteen months. The frustrations and tensions of that period dominated U.S. thinking and set the stage for Carter's election defeat. Ironically, the hostages were released just minutes after Carter had left the presidency, leading some to suggest that the incoming President had made a deal with the Iranians.

This assertion was a symptom of things to come. Carter's idealistic policies were interpreted by many as weak and ineffectual. His defeat heightened the conflict between liberal and conservative ideas, which would increase a deep, often bitter, division in American politics.

The Carters returned to Plains but continued their worldwide humanitarian work into their senior years. They joined work crews building homes for poor people through Habitat for Humanity and traveled on personal diplomatic missions to global trouble spots. In 1994, Carter helped negotiate the departure of Haiti's dictator preparatory to the U.S.-backed installation of the democratically-elected president. Carter wrote more than a dozen books on world peace, government, and faith, outlining his ideas for bringing a better life to humanity.

Rosalynn Smith Carter

Born Aug. 18, 1927, Plains, Ga.
Children: **3 sons, 1 daughter**

Accomplishments:
**Worked as managing partner in family businesses.
Actively campaigned for her husband.
Conducted diplomatic missions.
Aided programs for mental health & elderly.
Honorary Chairperson of President's Commission on Mental Health, 1977-78.
Worked with husband in Habitat for Humanity.**

Left: *President Anwar Sadat of Egypt (left) shakes hands with Prime Minister Menachem Begin of Israel (right), as Jimmy Carter looks on. In a triumph of personal diplomacy, Carter arranged the historic meeting between the old antagonists at the presidential retreat, Camp David, in September, 1978. The breakthrough Camp David accords established a framework for peace in the Middle East and led to a treaty between Israel and Egypt.*

Above: *Rosalynn Carter gazes appreciatively at her husband during his acceptance speech at the 1980 Democratic Convention. Rosalynn's confidence in her husband was communicated to others in a gracious, warm manner, enhancing her effectiveness as a campaigner. The ties of love binding the Carters were touchingly expressed in Jimmy Carter's 1994 book,* Always a Reckoning, *in which he wrote of his tender feelings for his long-time partner.*

RONALD REAGAN

FORTIETH PRESIDENT
1981-1989
NANCY DAVIS REAGAN

Ronald Wilson Reagan

In Office
Jan. 20, 1981-Jan. 20, 1989
Born Feb. 6, 1911, Tampico, Ill.
Party: **Republican**

Other Offices:
President, Screen Actors Guild, 1947-60.
Governor of California, 1967-75

Marriages:
Jane Wyman (Sarah Jane Fulks) Reagan, 1940, married 9 yrs., 1 son, 1 daughter with Reagan. Nancy Davis Reagan, 1952

Presidential Acts:
Initiated largest tax cuts in history, 1981.
Appointed first woman justice to the U.S. Supreme Court, 1981.
Urged development of Strategic Defense Initiative ("Star Wars"), 1983.
Authorized U.S. invasion of Grenada, 1983.
Attended controversial wreath-laying at Bitburg Cemetery, W. Germany, 1985.
Met Premier Gorbachev at Geneva Summit, 1985.
Authorized air strike against Libya, 1986.
Signed thorough revision of tax code, 1986.
Survived Iran-Contra Scandal, 1986-87.
Met Gorbachev to sign nuclear weapons reduction treaty, 1987.
Increased national debt to highest level in history.

Ronald Reagan was an actor who played the role of his life for eight years—President of the United States. Congenial and charming, Reagan was a master of human relationships, and many Americans loved him greatly, calling him "the Great Communicator." A conservative, he advocated restricting the government role in the national economy, reducing taxes, and decreasing regulations. After his first term, he sought reelection and carried forty-nine states. His great popularity was based on his assertion of patriotism and national pride, while his opponents considered him to be unintelligent and a destructive force in the country. Reagan's partner in the White House was his wife Nancy, a former actress who was also poised in public life.

HOLLYWOOD DAYS

Ronald Reagan was born in Tampico, Illinois. He attended local schools and worked in nearby Dixon as a lifeguard for five summers, saving seventy-seven people from drowning. The town put up a plaque in his honor. He worked his way through Eureka College, where he studied economics and sociology, played football, acted in college plays, and was president of the student body. Combining his interests in sports and acting, he became a radio sports announcer and acquired a national reputation. He took a screen test, and Warner Brothers Studios signed him up.

He made his movie debut in 1937 in *Love is in the Air*, playing a smalltown radio announcer exposing corrupt local politicians. He gained a following with his 1940 portrayal of George Gipp, the football player, in *Knute Rockne—All American*. In later years, he used a sentimental phrase from that movie for himself: "Let's win one for the Gipper." In all, Reagan appeared in more than fifty movies and was elected President of the Screen Actors Guild for five consecutive terms.

He was first married to the well-known film actress Jane Wyman, with whom he had two children, Maureen and Michael. Their marriage ended after nine years; Reagan was the only president to have been divorced. A few years later, Reagan married actress Nancy Davis. Born in New York, Nancy grew up in Chicago with her mother and stepfather. Nancy majored in theater at Smith College and appeared on Broadway and in eleven films.

She met Reagan through the Screen Actors Guild and married him in March, 1952. Their daughter Patricia (Patti Davis) was born in October, 1952, and their son Ronald in 1958. Both children later became professional performers. In 1957, the Reagans starred together in their last film, *Hellcats of the Navy*. Reagan became General Electric's public relations representative, and Nancy retired from professional life to become "the wife I wanted to be."

Left: *President Ronald Reagan delivers the State of the Union address to Congress in 1985. Reagan shifted from a career in acting to prominence in politics without missing a beat. An advocate of fiscal conservatism, he cut funding for key environmental and social programs but expanded spending in other areas.*

Left: *Ronald Reagan and Alexis Smith starred in the 1947 movie* Stallion Road, *the first commercial film Reagan made after wartime service making Army training films. Reagan played a Southern California veterinarian who treats a sick horse and falls in love with the blonde owner.*

MOVE TO CONSERVATISM

Originally a Democrat, Reagan switched to the Republican party in 1962, and in 1964 he delivered a nationally televised speech for conservative presidential candidate Barry Goldwater. The speech was well received and convinced Reagan he might have a future in politics. In 1967, he was sworn in as California Governor—a post he held for two terms. The country's economic problems and the Iranian hostage crisis made President Carter vulnerable, and the Republicans nominated Reagan for president. Reagan won the 1980 election handily—at sixty-nine, the oldest man ever elected president.

Reagan was in office only two months when an assassin nearly killed him. A deranged gunman attacked the President outside the Washington Hilton, wounding him and his press secretary, James Brady, as well as two others. All of those shot survived the attack, but Brady was left with serious disabilities. Brady and his wife Sarah became ardent supporters of gun control, but for some time Reagan did not.

Below: Nancy Reagan signs autographs at an anti-drug rally in Harper's Ferry, West Virginia. The First Lady spearheaded the campaign against drug and alcohol abuse among the nation's young people. Her slogan, "Just Say No," became widely known all across the country, encouraging young people to reject the use of narcotics and alcohol.

Reagan and his colleagues cut back many environmental and social welfare programs but increased spending in other areas, such as a huge military buildup. "Reaganomics"—the administration's favorite economic policies—pleased conservatives but drove liberals to distraction. The economy went through increased decline before it greatly improved, while the deficit increased from $914 billion to $2.6 trillion. The U.S., once the world's largest creditor, became a major debtor nation. Reagan blamed Congress for the deficit, but Congressionally-added spending increased Reagan's own budget proposals by only one-fourteenth.

In foreign affairs, Reagan sent troops into the Caribbean island of Granada and aided right-wingers in El Salvador and Nicaragua. He spoke harshly against the Soviets, and the two nations engaged in proxy confrontations in many places. Reagan proposed the "Star Wars" initiative, a laser-beam defensive shield, to counter the "evil empire" of the Soviets. Many opposed the project on the basis of its huge projected costs, and experts doubted it would be effective.

THE SECOND TERM

Reagan was reelected by a landslide and in his second term became somewhat mellower. When Soviet leader Mikhail Gorbachev proposed an era of open relationships, the leaders met at four superpower summit meetings. They signed sweeping arms control agreements and established a pleasant cordiality.

The Iran-Contra scandal of 1986 revealed that the administration had been secretly selling arms to Iran in exchange for its assistance in freeing American hostages held in Lebanon. Further, money from this secret deal was diverted to the Nicaraguan right-wing paramilitary *contras.* Reagan denied knowing anything about this illegal arrangement, and through his remarkably successful geniality, slipped through the scandal unscathed.

Nancy Reagan exhibited a stylish sociability in the White House. She wore designer clothing and invited guests to lavish entertainments. She led the campaign against the use of illegal drugs

Nancy Davis (Anne Frances Robbins) Reagan

Born July 6, 1921, New York, N.Y.
***Children:* 1 daughter, 1 son**

Accomplishments:
Acted in stage and screen productions.
Supported her husband's work.
Advocated anti-drug abuse programs.
Worked with Foster Grandparent Program and other causes.

and popularized the slogan, "Just Say No." Reports indicated that Nancy's influence on her husband was extensive in both personal and political matters. She sometimes consulted astrologers to determine the best course of action for the President.

All in all, the Reagan duo performed well in their long-running appearance on the White House stage. The audience was highly appreciative; when Reagan left office, opinion polls showed him to be the most popular president since Franklin D. Roosevelt.

The Reagans retired to California, and a few years later, the former president revealed that he had become a victim of Alzheimer's Disease, which causes mental degeneration. The public responded sympathetically to this courageous admission and wished the Reagans well.

Left: Ronald and Nancy Reagan wave as they embark on a helicopter trip from the White House to the presidential retreat at Camp David. The Reagans enjoyed a deep bond of true friendship and interdependence, and the president's performance in office directly benefited from his wife's counsel

Left: The Blue Room at the White House looked like this during Reagan's presidency. It was redecorated by Pat Nixon and was not altered again until 1995. Memories of weddings, funerals, concerts, and receptions have wafted through the graceful oval room for two centuries.

Right: George Bush accepts the presidential nomination at the 1988 Republican National Convention in New Orleans. Bush had a record of solid experience as Vice President, CIA Director, and envoy to the United Nations and China, and the nation looked to him for leadership.

George Herbert Walker Bush

In Office
Jan.20, 1989-Jan. 20, 1993
Born June 12, 1924,
Milton, Mass.
Party: **Republican**

Other Offices:
U.S. Navy pilot, Lt. jg., 1942-45.
U.S. Congressman, 1967-71.
U.S. Ambassador to the United Nations, 1971-72.
Chief, U.S. Liaison Office, Peking, 1974-75.
Director, Central Intelligence Agency, 1976-77.
Vice President, 1981-89.

Marriage:
Barbara Pierce Bush, 1945, married more than 50 yrs.

Presidential Acts:
Dealt with savings & loan crisis, Los Angeles riots, environmental crises.
Guided U.S. during period of Eastern European revolutions and breakup of Soviet Union, 1989-90.
Met with Russian leaders, signed disarmament treaties.
Ousted Gen. Noriega from Panama, 1989.
Organized international coalition to defeat Iraq in Persian Gulf War, 1991.
Sent U.S. troops to famine-struck Somalia, 1992.

GEORGE BUSH

FORTY-FIRST PRESIDENT
1989-1993
BARBARA PIERCE BUSH

George Bush was elected to the presidency after having been vice president for eight years under President Reagan. He provided steady leadership at a time of important changes on the international and domestic scene. He skillfully dealt with important challenges, and yet the voters failed to reelect him. His wife Barbara achieved remarkable popularity with her unaffected manner—many felt they could relate to her as they might to their own mother or grandmother.

FAMILY AND POLITICS

Both George and Barbara Bush were children of privileged homes. George was one of four offspring of Prescott Bush, a successful businessman and Wall Street investor who represented Connecticut in the Senate for a decade. George spent his childhood in Greenwich, Connecticut, one of the country's most expensive communities. At Phillips Academy, he was a good student, athlete, and president of the senior class.

In 1941, young George met Barbara Pierce at a Christmas dance. Barbara was one of four children of the publisher of *McCall's* and *Redbook* magazines and grew up comfortably in Rye, a wealthy New York suburb. George spotted her across the dance floor, arranged a meeting, and became the first boy ever to give pretty sixteen-year-old Barbara a kiss.

George named his bomber plane "Barbara" after her. He was then the youngest pilot in the Navy. He flew dangerous missions against Japan in the Pacific and was awarded the Distinguished Flying Cross.

Barbara dropped out of Smith College to marry George in 1945. Bush attended Yale, where he majored in economics and graduated Phi Beta Kappa. During their many years together, the couple occupied twenty-nine homes in seventeen cities and had six children. They suffered grief when their three-year-old daughter died of leukemia. Barbara's hair turned white at that time, and she has worn it proudly since.

Bush entered the Texas oil business at the bottom and worked his way up to president of a major off-shore drilling company. Active in Republican affairs, he was elected to Congress, where he courageously voted for the 1968 Civil Rights Act, guaranteeing equal housing opportunities.

He failed in a bid for the Senate, but Nixon appointed him United Nations Ambassador, and Ford chose him as Chairman of the Republican National Committee, Chief of the U.S. Liaison Office in China and Director of the CIA, where he restored agency morale. As Reagan's vice president, he logged more than a million miles of diplomatic travel and was briefly Acting President while Reagan underwent intestinal surgery. His role in the Iran-Contra Affair is unclear.

FAST-CHANGING SCENE

In 1988, Bush successfully campaigned for the presidency, calling for a conservative program and a "kinder, and gentler nation." Soon after taking office, Bush faced a long-developing crisis in the savings and loan industry, which eventually cost the country hundreds of billions of dollars. Concern for the environment increased with a giant oil spill from the *Exxon Valdez* in Alaska, and the economy went into recession. Riots broke out in Los Angeles, and Bush had to send in federal troops to restore order.

Bush took bold military action in Panama in 1989, ordering in U.S. troops to overthrow the dictatorship of General Manuel Noriega, who was later jailed on charges of drug trafficking. In the most dramatic phase of his presidency, Bush sent hundreds of thousands of troops to the Middle East to fight Iraq's invasion of oil-rich Kuwait. He was able to enlist the active support of several nations, including Saudi Arabia, in the fight against Iraq. In a sweeping campaign, "Operation Desert Storm," Iraq was driven back, and Bush gained enormous prestige.

Relationships with the former Soviet bloc underwent dramatic transformation, as the Soviet Union split apart and formerly communist nations set up democratic governments. Bush met with Soviet Premier Gorbachev and President Boris Yeltsin in a series of summits in which important nuclear-weapon reduction treaties were signed and U.S.-Russian relationships were completely restructured.

Barbara Bush enjoyed organizing White House functions and spending time with her five grown children and their families. Her volunteer work was extensive, with her greatest focus on the promotion of literacy. Her book on Millie, their springer spaniel, became a best seller. She authored a 1994 memoir of her experiences which was also well-received.

As the economy, crime, and homelessness in the United States worsened, the public which had so admired Bush for his skillful handling of international dangers turned against him and voted him out of office. The Bushes retired with dignity to private life in Texas. They continued to enjoy holidays at their beloved seashore home at Kennebunkport, Maine.

Above: The joy of reunion delights a Navy fighter pilot greeting his two-year-old daughter after his two-and-a-half month deployment to the Persian Gulf. The April, 1991, homecoming followed a speedy victory over the Iraqi invaders of Kuwait.

Above: Barbara Bush addresses a campaign rally, using her delightful personality to win votes for her husband. Despite a privileged background, Barbara always had the common touch, and people loved her for her genuineness. She worked to assist the cause of combating illiteracy in America and once said that she "tries to do some good every day."

Barbara Pierce Bush

Born June 8, 1925, Bronx, N.Y.
Children: **4 sons, 2 daughters (1 daughter died)**

Accomplishments:
Raised large family, coordinated complex household. Volunteered for United Negro College Fund, Leukemia Society, March of Dimes, Literacy Volunteers of America. Established Barbara Bush Foundation for Family Literacy.

Right: President Bill Clinton announces a change in his Cabinet at a 1994 White House press conference. Clinton came into office promising a return to enlightened liberal governmental policies but met difficulties in making good on his pledges. His own ideals conflicted with those of the Republican-dominated Congress sworn in at the beginning of 1995.

William Jefferson Clinton

In Office: Jan. 20, 1993-
Born Aug. 19, 1946, Hope, Ark.
***Party:* Democratic**

Other Offices:
Arkansas Attorney General, 1977-79.
Governor of Arkansas, 1979-81, 1983-92.

Marriage:
Hillary Rodham Clinton, 1975.

Presidential Acts:
Ordered U.S. aid to former Yugoslavian republic of Bosnia-Herzegovina, 1993.
Proposed economic plan to reduce budget deficit, 1993.
Supported NAFTA trading pact, 1993.
Sponsored key anticrime bill, 1994.
Withdrew U.S. forces from Somalia, 1994, 1995.
Sent assistance to Rwandan refugees, 1994.
Dealt with Cuban Refugee Crisis, Haitian Crisis, 1994-95.
Attempted to solve U.S. Health Care Crisis.
Struggled to reduce federal deficit left by predecessors.

WILLIAM (BILL) CLINTON

FORTY-SECOND PRESIDENT 1993-

HILLARY RODHAM CLINTON

Bill Clinton's rise to the presidency revealed that even in the late twentieth century, one could still live the classic American dream. Bill was born in the little town of Hope, Arkansas, to a recently-widowed mother and raised by an alcoholic stepfather who abused Bill's mother. Making the most of his educational opportunities, Clinton studied at Georgetown University and, as a Rhodes Scholar, at Oxford University. He studied law at Yale, and went on to become Governor of his home state before attaining America's highest political office.

Aiding Clinton in his rise to the top were two women—his mother, Virginia, a nurse who imbued him with a sense of compassion and justice, and his wife, Hillary, who offered indispensible advice and assistance throughout his political career.

AN ACTIVIST COUPLE

Originally named William Jefferson Blythe IV after the father he never met—he was killed in a car accident three months before Bill was born—Bill later took the last name of his stepfather, Roger Clinton, a car dealer.

Bill honed his political abilities in school elections, and at the age of seventeen was sent to Washington, D.C., as a delegate to the American Legion Boys Nation. There he shook hands with President John F. Kennedy, a moment that was "an inspiration that burned into the mind and soul."

At Yale Law School Clinton met fellow law student Hillary Rodham, a remarkably bright and energetic young woman. Hillary grew up in Park Ridge, Illinois, a Chicago suburb, as the daughter of a drapery-maker and a homemaker. An excellent student, Hillary was a National Merit Scholarship finalist. At Wellesley College, she was president of the student government and delivered the school's first student commencement address. At Yale Law School, she pondered how to combine social activism and a legal career. Inspired by black lawyer Marian Wright Edelman, Hillary's focus became the rights of children to education and medical care.

Hillary became an acclaimed young attorney and received job offers from numerous major law firms. She shocked friends when she elected to join Bill Clinton on the law faculty of the University of Arkansas. The couple married in 1975 and joined together in a combined career of political and social activism. Bill served five terms as Governor of Arkansas, while Hillary developed a substantial legal practice and worked to improve the state's educational system. Their daughter Chelsea was born in 1980.

Clinton's campaign for the presidency was marred by allegations of draft-dodging, protesting the Vietnam war, and marital infidelity. The Clintons appeared on television's *Sixty Minutes* to reveal that they had indeed come through marital difficulties successfully, and that issue seemed to fall away. Clinton attacked the policies of his opponents, George Bush and independent candidate Ross Perot, and was elected president.

AT HOME AND ABROAD

The third-youngest man to take office, Clinton faced an abundance of foreign and domestic problems. Bloody fighting in the former Yugoslavia defied peace-making efforts, and the U.S. military mission to aid starving people in Somalia ran into serious difficulties. Historic agreements between the leaders of Israel, the Palestinians, and Jordan promised peace but were followed by continuing strife. Combining diplomacy and a strong threat of military force, Clinton ousted Haiti's brutal dictator and placed Haiti's democratically-elected president in power.

Clinton achieved a major policy goal with the approval of the North American Free Trade Agreement (NAFTA), liberalizing trading with Canada and Mexico. Hillary Clinton coordinated a massive effort to restructure the troubled national health care system, but the resulting proposals did not meet widespread approval.

The sharp focus on Hillary by the press and the public has reflected today's ambivalent attitudes toward the changing roles of women in American society. As First Lady, Hillary has represented the multiple aspirations of American womanhood yet has met harsh criticism. She is a committed mother as well as a gracious, well-dressed hostess overseeing redecorating plans at the White House, and is a talented, engaged professional woman seeking the best for her family and her country.

As Bill Clinton's presidential term proceeded, he struggled with a powerful Congress opposed to his visions of what was right for the country. In facing contention, the Clintons were like nearly every President and First Lady who had come before them, encountering honest disagreement within the lawfully mandated structures of a great democratic society, searching to find a way to shape and renew the nation in a continuing progression toward the promise of the future.

Below: Hillary Rodham Clinton meets media representatives at a 1994 dinner for radio and television correspondents. A well-educated woman of high intelligence and energy, Hillary acts as her husband's closest adviser. During the first years of her husband's presidency, Hillary Clinton gained a reputation as the most activist First Lady since Eleanor Roosevelt.

Hillary Rodham Clinton

Born Oct. 26, 1947, Chicago, Ill.
Children: **1 daughter**

Accomplishments:
**Taught at University of Arkansas Law School.
Practiced law successfully at Rose Law Firm, Little Rock, Ark.
Acted as Chair of Arkansas Educational Standards Committee, 1983.
Actively involved in numerous legal and social welfare organizations.
Headed Administration Task Force on Health Care Reform, 1993-94.
Acted as key adviser to her husband in all professional & political matters.**

Above: Balmy sea breezes cool the Clintons and the Kennedys at Martha's Vineyard off the coast of Massachusetts in August, 1993. Among those on the sailboat are, from left, President Bill Clinton (light knit shirt), Senator Ted Kennedy (standing and waving), Caroline Kennedy Schlossberg (sitting, with glasses and pony tail), First Lady Hillary Clinton (standing, with straw hat), former First Lady Jacqueline Kennedy Onassis (striped shirt), and Chelsea Clinton (sitting).

INDEX

*Page numbers in **bold face** type indicate picture captions*

REFERENCES

Aiken, Lonnelle. 1978. *The Living White House.* The White House Historical Association, with the National Geographic Society, Washington, D.C.

Anthony, Carl Sferrazza. 1990. *First Ladies; The Saga of the Presidents' Wives and Their Power, 1789-1961.* William Morrow & Co, Inc., New York.

Bassett, Margaret. 1969. *Profiles and Portraits of American Presidents and Their Wives.* With an introduction by Henry F. Graff. Bond Wheelwright Co., Freeport, Maine.

Beard, Charles A., updated by W. Beard and D. Vagts. 1989. *The Presidents in American History; George Washington to George Bush.* Julian Messner, Englewood Cliffs, N.J.

Boller, Paul F., Jr. 1981. *Presidential Anecdotes.* Oxford University Press, New York.

Boller, Paul F., Jr. 1988. *Presidential Wives: An Anecdotal History.* Oxford University Press, New York.

Crompton, Samuel. 1993. *The Presidents of the United States.* Smithmark Publishers, Inc., New York.

DeGregorio, William A. 1989. *The Complete Book of U.S. Presidents,* 2nd ed. Dember Books, New York.

Freidel, Frank. 1981. *The Presidents of the United States of America.* White House Historical Association & National Geographic Society, Washington, D.C.

Graham, Judith, ed. 1993. *Current Biography Yearbook, 1993.* H.W. Wilson Co., New York.

Hay, Peter. 1988. *All the Presidents' Ladies; Anecdotes of the Women Behind the Men in the White House.* Penguin Books, New York.

Healy, Diana Dixon. 1988. *America's First Ladies; Private Lives of the Presidential Wives.* Atheneum, New York.

Hilton, George S. 1899. *The Funny Side of Politics.* New York.

Kane, Joseph Nathan. 1989. *Facts About the Presidents.* Fifth Edition. H.W. Wilson Co., New York.

Klapthor, Margaret Brown. 1981, 1989. *The First Ladies.* White House Historical Association & National Geographic Society, Washington, D.C.

Klapthor, Margaret Brown, et. al. 1982. *The First Ladies Cook Book.* GMG Publishing, New York.

Kunhardt, Philip B., Jr., P.B. Kunhardt III, and P.W. Kunhardt. 1992. *Lincoln; An Illustrated Biography.* Alfred A. Knopf, New York.

Leish, Kenneth W., ed. 1968. *The American Heritage Pictorial History of the Presidents of the United States.* 2 vols. American Heritage Publishing Co., Inc.

Leish, Kenneth W., and the Editors of the Newsweek Book Division. 1972. *The White House.* Newsweek, New York.

Lindsay, Rae. 1989. *The Presidents' First Ladies.* Franklin Watts, New York.

McClure, A.K. n.d. *Lincoln's Own Yarns and Stories.* Chicago.

Poore, Benjamin. 1886. *Perley's Reminiscences of Sixty Years.* New York.

Post, Robert C., et. al. 1984. *Every Four Years.* Smithsonian Books, Distributed by W.W. Norton & Co., New York.

Reeves, Thomas C. 1975. *Gentleman Boss: The Life of Chester Alan Arthur.* Alfred A. Knopf, New York.

Seale, William. 1986. *The President's House; A History.* 2 vols. White House Historical Association, with the National Geographic Society, Washington, D.C., and Harry N. Abrams, Inc., New York.

The World Book Encyclopedia. 1980, 1995. 22 vols. World Book, Inc., Chicago.

Wright, John W., ed. 1994. *The Universal Almanac, 1995.* Andrews & McMeel, Kansas City.